Gifted

Christopher Cone

Understanding the Holy Spirit and Unwrapping Spiritual Gifts

*Gifted: Understanding the Holy Spirit
And Unwrapping Spiritual Gifts*

©2015 Christopher Cone

Published by Exegetica Publishing
Ft. Worth, TX

ISBN10 – 0976593084

ISBN13 – 978-0-9765930-8-9

All rights reserved. No part of this publication may be reproduced, stored in a retrieval system, or transmitted in any form or by any means – electronic, mechanical, photocopy, recording, or any other – except for brief quotation in printed reviews, without the prior permission of the publisher.

All Scripture quotations, except those noted otherwise are from the New American Standard Bible, ©1960,1962,1963,1968,1971,1972,1973,1975, 1977, and 1995 by the Lockman Foundation.

Table of Contents

1. Gifted by God, Gifted with God 5
2. The Holy Spirit is a Person 7
3. The Holy Spirit Works 11
4. The Ministry of the Holy Spirit in Christ 15
5. Some Historical Perspectives 21
6. The Baptism of the Holy Spirit 29
7. The Role of the Holy Spirit in Our Understanding 35
8. Do We Value God's Communication? 49
9. Five Introductory Concepts 53
10. Does Every Believer Have a Spiritual Gift? 59
11. Identifying Spiritual Gifts 63
12. I Can't Help…I Don't Have That Gift 69
13. Gifts of Pastoring, Apostleship, and Evangelism? 73
14. The Peter Principles 79
15. What is Speaking in Tongues? Part 1 83
16. What is Speaking in Tongues? Part 2 95
17. Does Tongues Prove We Have the Holy Spirit? 101
18. On Possibility and Certainty 107
19. Purpose, and the Corinthians' Use of Tongues 117
20. Does God Speak to Us Today? 121
21. Does God Still Heal? 127

22. The Modern Dream Phenomena 129
23. The Nature of Prophecy 135
24. Are Revelatory Gifts for Today? 141
25. Eternal Security, the Holy Spirit, and Ethics 151
26. How Shall We Then Live? 157
Epilogue. The Importance of How We Interpret 163

1

Gifted by God, Gifted with God

It is understandable that Christians might focus on various giftings and enablement which were given to us for doing well in the Christian life. After all, we have every spiritual blessing in the heavenlies in Christ.[1] So there is indeed much we have been given, and there is much about which we need to learn. But we need to be careful not to miss the point of it all. If we focus only on the *gifts* God has given us, we might not draw into sharp enough focus the *gift* God has given us in Himself. Imagine if someone invited you to a birthday party. You came bearing a gift for the host whose birthday it was. The host received your gift, and was so enjoying the gift that they forgot to thank you – forgot to acknowledge you at all, and you found yourself all alone as the host went off to enjoy the gift you gave. Most would consider that rude. At the very least it would not be an ideal way to treat a guest – let alone a generous guest.

In a similar way God has given us many gifts and many blessings, and we should be filled with thanksgiving. We should make giving thanks a significant

---
[1] Eph 1:3.

part of our communication to Him. Further, in our enjoying of those gifts, we need to recognize an important basis of those gifts – the gift of the Holy Spirit. God has not just given us spiritual gifts, but He has given us His own Spirit, just like He has given us His own Son.

There are three very important implications of the Holy Spirit's being given to us. First, in Ephesians 1:14 and 2 Corinthians 1:22 we discover that the Holy Spirit was given to us as a pledge, guarantee, or down payment of our inheritance in Christ. In other words, the Holy Spirit is given to every believer at the moment he or she believes in Jesus Christ, guaranteeing that every believer is secure in Christ.

Second, Romans 5:5 describes that "...the love of God has been poured out within our hearts through the Holy Spirit who was given to us." He is the vehicle through whom God demonstrates His love within us. It is in Him we have our security, and it is in Him we can walk and bear fruit (as we see in Galatians 5, for example).

Third, in 1 John 3:24 we are told that the assurance of our security in Christ comes by the Holy Spirit – we know we are in Him "by this, that He abides in us, by the Spirit Whom He has given." Our security is in Him, our walk is through Him, and our assurance is by Him. It is through the gift of the Holy Spirit that God provides us with every spiritual blessing in the heavenlies in Christ. Let's unwrap that gift, and understand who the Holy Spirit is and what He does in our lives.

2

The Holy Spirit Is a Person

The Bible teaches the existence of one God as three Persons: Father, Son, and Spirit.[2] Throughout the Hebrew Bible[3] God chooses often to refer to Himself in the plural as *elohim*. While the word *elohim* does at times refer to an individual member of the Godhead,[4] it is also a common reference to God in His fullness, indicative of both singularity and plurality. The Holy Spirit is identified interchangeably with *Yahweh*, the Hebrew name for God – another indicator of the deity of the Holy Spirit.[5]

In the Hebrew Bible only Psalm 51:11 and Isaiah 63:10-11 refer to the Spirit of God as *the Holy Spirit*, and in the Greek New Testament there are nearly one hundred references to the Spirit of God as the *Holy Spirit*.

---

[2] Compare Deut 6:4 with Is 48:12,16b; also see Mt 28:19 and Gal 4:6.

[3] Or, Old Testament.

[4] Ps 45:6; Heb. 1:8.

[5] Gen 1:2, 2 Sam 23:2-3, Ps 139:7, Is 6:9, Jer 23:24, 31:31-34, Mt 12:31-32, 28:19, Acts 5:3-4 28:25, 1 Cor 3:16, 6:19, 2 Cor 13:14, Eph 2:22, Heb 1:1 (2 Pet 1:21), 10:15.

In various terms the Holy Spirit is identified nearly three hundred times in the New Testament alone.

The Spirit is characterized as *holy*. The Hebrew term *qadesh* means "...separate, sacred, consecrated...as spoken of a man who devotes himself to God, and thus separates himself from the rest of the people."[6] The term could be understood simply as *wholly other*. The first time in Scripture God is called holy is done so by Himself in Leviticus 10:3 and 11:44-45. Isaiah 6:3 emphasizes three times that this is *the* characteristic most representative of who God is.

The Greek term, *hagios* means, "separate from common condition and use, holy,"[7] and is from the same root as *hagnos*, meaning "pure chaste modest, innocent, blameless."[8] The first three times *hagios* is used in the NT it refers specifically to the Holy Spirit. Revelation 4:8 repeats the term three times – as in Isaiah 6:3 – to indicate God's primary attribute: He is *holy*. If we could describe God using only one word, it would be *holy*.

The term spirit is translated from the Hebrew *ruach*, which refers broadly to "air in motion, blowing, wind, what is empty or transitory, spirit, mind, breath."[9] The first two mentions of *ruach* in the OT ascribe this to God,[10] and in over one hundred instances in the OT the

---

[6] Davidson, *The Analytical Hebrew and Chaldee Lexicon* (Peabody, MA: Hendrickson Publishers, 1981), 654.
[7] Mounce, *The Analytical Lexicon to the Greek New Testament* (Grand Rapids, MI: Zondervan, 1993), 50.
[8] Ibid, 51.
[9] Holladay, *A Concise Hebrew and Aramaic Lexicon of the Old Testament* (Grand Rapids, MI: Eerdmans Publishing, 1972), 334.
[10] Gen 1:2, 6:3.

term is used to reference the Holy Spirit of God. The Greek *pneuma* refers to "wind, air, motion"[11] and also spirit in contrast to flesh. The first five instances of *pneuma* in the NT refer directly to God.[12]

There are two vital concepts regarding the identity of the Holy Spirit: He is deity and He is a person.[13] Because He is God, the Holy Spirit possesses the attributes of God.[14] He is of the same essence as Father and Son, as He is referred to as God, though He is subordinate *in function* to the Father and Son, as He is sent by both of them.[15] While the Son's personality proclaims that of the Father, the Spirit's personality proclaims that of the Son.[16] He is distinct from the Father and Son, though intimately connected.[17]

Because He is a person, He is referred to with personal pronouns,[18] and He is described in terms

---

[11] Mounce, 379.
[12] Mt 1:18,20; 3:11,16; 4:1.
[13] Gen 1:2; 6:3; Num 11:29; Judg 3:10; Ps 139:7; Is 61:1; Mt 3:16; 10:20; Lk 4:18; Acts 5:9; 8:39; 16:7; Rom 8:9, 11; 1 Cor 2:11; 3:3, 16; 6:11, 19-20; 2 Cor 3:17-18; Gal 4:6; Php 1:19; 1 Pet 1:11.
[14] Including holiness (Ps 51:1; Mt 1:20; Lk 11:13; Rom 1:4), omnipotence (Gen 1:2), wisdom and understanding (Ex 28:3, Is 11:2), omnipresence (Ps. 139:7), grace (Zech 12:10, Heb 10:29), truth (Jn 14:17, Acts 5:1-11, 1 Jn 5:6), life (Rom 8:2), omniscience (1 Cor 2:10-11), lordship (2 Cor 3:18), love (Gal 5:22, 1 Jn 4:8), faithfulness (1 Cor 1:9, 10:13, Gal 5:22, 1 Pet 4:19), unity and uniqueness (1 Cor 12:4-6, Eph 4:4), eternality (Heb 9:14), and glory (1 Pet 4:14).
[15] Ps 104:30, Is 48:16, Jn 14:16, 14:26, 15:26, Gal 4:6, Rom 8:9.
[16] Jn 16:13-14.
[17] Mt 3:16-17, 28:29, Lk 3:21-22, Jn 16:14, 17:4, 2 Cor 13:14, Jude 21.
[18] E.g., Jn 15:26, 16:13-14, Acts 13:2.

consistent with personhood. He speaks,[19] He can be insulted,[20] He can be blasphemed,[21] He can be resisted,[22] He can be grieved,[23] He can be lied to,[24] He strives,[25] He teaches,[26] He regenerates,[27] He convicts,[28] He helps and intercedes,[29] He possesses power,[30] He is distinct from power,[31] He knows,[32] He gives gifts,[33] He moves men,[34] He sanctifies,[35] He empowers,[36] and He prefers.[37]

---

[19] Acts 2:4, 8:29, 10:19-20, 13:2, 16:6-7, 21:11; 1 Tim. 4:1.
[20] Heb 10:29.
[21] Mt 12:31.
[22] Acts 7:51.
[23] Is 63:10, Eph 4:30.
[24] Acts 5:3-4.
[25] Gen 6:3.
[26] Lk 12:12.
[27] Jn 3:8, Rom 8:11.
[28] Jn 16:8.
[29] Jn 16:7, Rom 8:26.
[30] Lk 1:35, 4:14, Rom 15:13,19.
[31] Acts 10:38, 1 Cor 2:4.
[32] 1 Cor 2:10-11.
[33] 1 Cor 12:4, 8-11.
[34] 2 Pet 1:21.
[35] 1 Pet 1:2.
[36] "Comes upon," Num 11:25, 24:2, Judg 3:10, 6:34, 11:29, 14:6,15:14, 1 Sam 10:10, 11:6, 16:13, 19:20-23, 1 Ch 12:18, 2 Ch 20:14.
[37] Acts 15:28.

3

The Holy Spirit Works

The Holy Spirit does the work of God in the world – with unbelievers and with believers. He was actively involved in creation.[38] He strives, restrains, and convicts.[39] He was involved in the communication and preservation of God's word,[40] guiding the apostles into the truth they needed in order to recount and record the things that took place.[41] He gives believers the tools they need to understand and receive or accept His word.[42]

Jesus describes the Holy Spirit as another Helper,[43] using the Greek word *allon,* meaning another of the same kind as opposed to *heteron,* meaning another of a different kind. This Helper would be of the same kind as Jesus. Both would intercede on our behalf.[44] The two are intimately connected, yet distinct – the Holy Spirit was even involved in the human conception of Jesus.[45]

---

[38] Gen 1:2, Job 26:13, 33:4; Ps 33:6; 104:30.
[39] Gen 6:3, Jn 16:7-11, 2 Thes 2:6-8.
[40] Eph 6:17, 2 Tim 3:15-17, 2 Pet 1:20-21.
[41] Jn 16:12-15.
[42] 1 Cor 2:9-12, contrasted with 2 Cor 4:3-4.
[43] Jn 14:26.
[44] Rom 8:26-27, 34.
[45] Lk 1:35.

The ministry of the Holy Spirit to believers during the church age is different from His ministry during the time of the Old Testament. Then, He would fill or come upon people to help them accomplish what God intended.[46] He continued that filling up ministry even from the time of Christ's earthly ministry into the early church – particularly with the apostles.[47] He still fills believers today, but in a different way than He did in Old Testament times.

During the church age the Holy Spirit provides new life and regeneration to those who have believed in Christ,[48] He baptizes believers into the body of Christ.[49] He sanctifies, or sets apart believers.[50] He seals them for the day of redemption,[51] and He indwells believers always.[52] Having all these blessings – and unlike Old Testament believers – church age believers are actually *commanded* to be filled with the Holy Spirit.[53] We can't have more of the Holy Spirit than we already do – He indwells us fully. But we can be more controlled by Him by filling ourselves with His word and subjecting ourselves to the work He is doing in us. To be filled with

---

[46] Ex 31:3, 35:31, Deut 34:9, Ezek 43:5, Mic 3:8.
[47] Lk 1:15, 41, 67, Acts 2:4, 4:8, 31, 9:17, 13:9.
[48] Mt 19:28, 1 Cor 15:24-28, Tit 3:5, Jn 3:6, 10:10, 2 Cor. 5:17, 1 Pet. 1:23.
[49] Mt 3:11, Mk 1:8, Lk 3:16, Jn 1:33, Acts 1:5 (2:2-3), 11:16, Rom 6:1-4, 1 Cor 12:13, Gal 3:27, Eph 4:5, Col 2:12, Tit. 3:5.
[50] 2 Thes 2:13.
[51] Eph 1:13-14, 4:30.
[52] Jn 7:37-39, Acts 11:17, Rom 5:5, 8:9-11, 1Cor 2:12, 3:16, 6:19-20, 12:13, 2 Cor 5:5, Gal 3:2, 4:6, Eph 2:22, 2 Tim 1:14, Jam 4:5, 1 Jn 3:24, 4:13.
[53] Eph 5:17-21.

the Holy Spirit in the church age is to be *controlled* by the Holy Spirit. That is why Paul tells believers, in Ephesians 5:17-19, not to be drunk with wine, but instead to be filled by the Holy Spirit. In the same way that when we fill ourselves with wine, that wine controls us, we should fill ourselves with His word, and allow ourselves to be controlled by Him. Notice in Ephesians 5:18 the imperative *to be filled* is in the passive voice. We are commanded to be filled, but He is the one that does the filling. We need to be subject to it. Just as Romans 12:2 describes – we should be transformed by the renewing of our minds – a renewing that is all about the work of His word in our lives. This being filled by the Spirit is also related to walking by the Spirit, which is contrasted to walking in the flesh.[54] Being filled with and walking in the Spirit has a definite impact on the life of the believer, resulting in the Holy Spirit bearing fruit in the believer.[55]

---

[54] Gal 5:16.
[55] Gal 5:15-26.

14   Gifted

4

The Ministry of the Holy Spirit In Christ

While the Holy Spirit has an incredible ministry directly to believers, that is certainly not His only role. Before the Spirit's present ministry in the church, He also interacted with Christ in several profound ways. As we understand the relationship of Christ and the Spirit, and their relationship to the Father, we can be encouraged and strengthened, knowing that we also have a relationship with all Three, and that they are doing amazing things so that we can have life,[56] and walk with Him.[57]

His Purpose in Christ

The Holy Spirit *bore witness* to the fact that Christ was sent from the Father, and by so doing provided a testimony to Israel that Jesus was indeed the Messiah. Note the fourfold witness identified in John's gospel: (1) John[58] was the forerunner prophesied by the Holy Spirit,[59] (2) Jesus' works,[60] many of which were

---

[56] Eph 1:3-14.
[57] Jn 17:3.
[58] Jn 5:33-35.
[59] Mal 3:1, Lk. 1:67-79.

accomplished in the power of the Holy Spirit, (3) the Father[61] – through His word, which is the sword of the Spirit,[62] and finally, (4) the Scriptures,[63] which are the words and testimony of the Spirit.[64] His words were provided by method of inspiration – or God breathing,[65] as He moved men to speak His word.[66]

The Holy Spirit's activity is present in each of the four witnesses to Jesus' authenticity. He also was intimately involved in Jesus' earthly life and ministry – particularly in fulfillment of prophecy, and bearing witness by truth and remembrance to the Person of Jesus the Christ.[67]

In The Conception of Christ in His Humanity

Isaiah 9:6-7 prophesied a child, a son, whom would be "Mighty God." While Christ is eternally the Son of God,[68] in His humanity Christ was conceived by the Holy Spirit,[69] leaving no doubt that Christ did not have imputed sin from Adam,[70] and that He was qualified as the seed of Eve[71] to take away the sin of humanity.

---

[60] Jn 5:36.
[61] Jn 5:37-38.
[62] Eph 6:17.
[63] Jn 5:39-47.
[64] Is 59:21, Zech 4:6, Acts 21:11, 1 Tim 4:1, Heb 3:7, 9:8, 10:15, Rev 2:7, 11, 17, 29, 3:6, 13, 22.
[65] 2 Tim 3:16.
[66] 2 Pet 1:20-21.
[67] Jn 14:26, 15:26, 16:13.
[68] Having nothing to do with origin, but everything to do with His rights and authority, see Col 1:15-19.
[69] Lk 1:35.
[70] Rom 5:12.
[71] Gen 3:15.

In The Anointing of Christ (As Upon Him)

The Hebrew *meshiyach* refers to the process of rubbing or pouring (as in oil) to indicate one who is consecrated,[72] appointed, or commissioned.[73] The Greek *chrio* describes the same action.[74] The anointing by the Spirit indicated several things: (1) Jesus' deity[75] as the covenant making, covenant keeping Yahweh,[76] (2) Jesus' acceptability and chosenness by God[77] in regards to His qualification as *the* Messiah, the Christ,[78] (3) Jesus' power,[79] (4) Jesus' kingship,[80] (5) Jesus' sonship,[81] (6) Jesus' rejection,[82] and (7) Jesus' authority to baptize in or by the Holy Spirit.[83]

In The Filling of Christ

Christ was filled with the Holy Spirit[84] and with power,[85] armed with the word of God to pronounce

---

[72] Benjamin Davidson, *The Analytical Hebrew and Chaldee Lexicon* (Peabody, MA: Hendrickson, 1995), 519.
[73] Brown, Driver, and Briggs, *A Hebrew and English Lexicon of the Old Testament* (Oxford, UK: Oxford University Press, 1906), 602-603.
[74] Bauer, Arndt, Gingrich, *A Greek-English Lexicon of the New Testament and Other Early Christian Literature*, 4th Revised and Augmented Edition (Chicago, IL: University of Chicago Press, 1952), 895-896.
[75] Ps 45:6.
[76] Is 61:1-2, 8, Lk 4:18-21.
[77] Is 42:1.
[78] Both *meshiyach* and *chrio* are forms of the Messianic title.
[79] Acts 10:38,
[80] Ps 2:2, 6, 45:6-7, Heb 1:9.
[81] Ps 2:2, 7, Mt 3:16-17, Mk 1:10-11, Lk 3:22.
[82] Ps 2:1-3, Acts 4:23-31.
[83] Jn 1:33.
[84] Lk 4:1.

judgment and to prove His perfection. Why did Jesus, the image of the invisible God and ruler over all[86] need to be filled with the Spirit? Had Jesus given up His deity at His incarnation? Was He in need of divine assistance due to some human limitation? Certainly not! The Holy Spirit of God filled Jesus Christ in *fulfillment of prophecy and as a testimony* to the identity of the incomparable Christ, demonstrating the identity of Jesus as the Messiah and as God.

In Rejoicing

Jesus rejoices in the Holy Spirit at the things done by the Father,[87] who had hidden things from the wise and revealed them to infants, as Jesus put it. Notice the joy of the Son in the Father, is expressed in the Spirit. In short, this context gives us a glimpse into the relationship of Father, Son, and Spirit, and shows us how the Three relate to each other.

In Testing

Immediately after the Holy Spirit's evidencing of Jesus' identity as the Son of God, the Spirit leads Jesus into temptation,[88] and yet it was the word of the Spirit which was Jesus' means of thwarting temptation. Again we see the Spirit providing confirmation of the perfections

---

[85] Mic 3:5,8, Lk 4:1.
[86] Col 1:15-19.
[87] Lk 10:21.
[88] Mt 4:1.

of Jesus the Christ, and aiding in the completion of Jesus' qualification as the faithful High Priest.[89]

In Miracles/Casting Out of Demons

The Holy Spirit was a part of Jesus' miracle working ministry, as an attestation that the Messiah had indeed come.[90] Ryrie explains the significance of this function: "He also gave sight to the blind because the Spirit was upon Him.[91] In the Old Testament giving sight to the blind was a prerogative of God[92] and something Messiah would do.[93] Thus when the Lord restored sight to blind people He was making a clear claim to be Israel's long awaited Messiah."[94] It is worth noting that Christ performed miracles both by the Spirit[95] and also in His own power.[96] Christ was deity, yet He worked in conjunction with the Holy Spirit to accomplish His particular purposes.

In His Death and Resurrection

In these remarkable works we see the very close relationship of Christ and the Holy Spirit. Neither were working independently, and they were both

---

[89] Heb 2:17-18.
[90] Mt 12:28,31, Mk 3:22-30, Lk 11:14-23.
[91] Lk 4:18.
[92] Ex 4:11, Ps 146:8.
[93] Is 29:18, 35:5, 42:7.
[94] Charles Ryrie, *Basic Theology* (Wheaton: IL, Victor, 1982), 350.
[95] Mt 12:28.
[96] Lk 5:17, Jn 18:6.

accomplishing tremendous things in the death and resurrection of Jesus Christ.[97]

Conclusion

In light of the testimony of the Holy Spirit in the life and ministry of Jesus Christ, when we are told that we are sealed by the Holy Spirit of God[98] and that the Holy Spirit of God bears witness that we are children of God,[99] that our position is secure and that we are in Him[100] – we can take Him at His word. We can *know* it to be true.

John wrote his Gospel as a testimony that we might know Jesus is the Christ, the Son of God, and that believing we may have life in His name.[101] John later writes his first epistle in order that we might know[102] that we have eternal life.[103] Because of the Holy Spirit's testimony in the life and ministry of Jesus Christ, no longer is our understanding of our position simply a matter of faith (of course it was granted to us by faith, and of course we are to walk in faith), it is also a matter of assuredness. We *know* it to be fact. He is the Covenant Keeping God who has taken the time not only to keep His promises, but to repeatedly demonstrate His faithfulness to us – the undeserving. Praise be to God for His holiness and His mercy!

---

[97] Rom 1:4, Heb 9:14, 1 Pet 3:18.
[98] Eph 1:14.
[99] Rom 8:16.
[100] Rom 8:9.
[101] Jn 20:30-31.
[102] To know factually, Greek, *eidete*, from *oidos*.
[103] 1 Jn 5:13.

5

Some Historical Perspectives On the Holy Spirit And His Ministry to Believers

Thinking through history can certainly be an arduous task at times. But like the wise saying goes, those that don't know history are doomed to repeat it. Historically there have been some remarkable disagreements regarding the Holy Spirit and His ministry in the church age. Many of these disagreements are resolved in the short term but then crop back up in later generations. Having a little bit of historical perspective can help us to recognize old errors when they freshly appear under new names. So let's just take a quick walk through two thousand years of history in understanding the Holy Spirit and His ministry. If you would rather not take that walk, feel free to sit on a bench and skip this chapter for now, but don't underestimate the value of a good walk.

Until Montanus (170 AD), the church as a whole neither emphasized nor defined the doctrine of the Holy Spirit. Montanus, along with two women (Prisca and Maximilla) claimed to have a prophetic ministry, ushering in what they called the Age of the Paraclete, involving supposed new revelation through the Holy Spirit. These claims, although ultimately rejected by most, forced the church to examine the doctrine of the Holy Spirit.

Monarchianism, arising during the late second century, promoted the idea that God was one person and not three persons in one trinity, and that He was the sole Monarch. This teaching later developed into two concepts: modalism and adoptionism. Modalism was a teaching popularized by Sabellius (215 AD), that there were three manifestations or modes of God, but not three persons. Adoptionism was the idea that Christ as man was only the son of God in the sense that He was adopted, He was not truly deity.

Sabellius viewed the trinity as economic, not immanent. He said, for example, that "God as united to the creation is Father; God as united to Jesus Christ is the Son; God united to the church is the Holy Spirit."[104] This view came to be known as modalism, as the Son and Holy Spirit are seen in this view to be simply modes of expression of God, and not distinct Persons. Sabellius' view also was referred to as Patripassianism,[105] specifically in relation to Christ, that God the Father suffered in human form as Jesus.

Arius, condemned by Council of Nicea (325 AD), said that God the Father creates and recreates the Son and Spirit, and that they are not divine or without beginning. Arius' views dealt most directly with

---

[104] Augustus Strong, *Systematic Theology* (Toronto, CA: University of Toronto, 1907), 327.
[105] From the Latin *patri*, father, and *passus*, to suffer.

Christology, but his views had significant implications on the doctrine of the Holy Spirit, as Arius taught that the Spirit was the first creation of Christ. In similar fashion, Macedonius (360 AD) taught that the Spirit was created by the Son, and therefore subordinate. The First Council of Constantinople (381 AD) dealt with Arian and Macedonian error in a fairly diplomatic statement that read as follows: "And we believe in the Holy Spirit, the Lord, the Life-giving, who proceeds from the Father, who is to be glorified with the Father and the son, and who speaks through the prophets."[106]

In 399 AD, there arose what was came to be known as the Anthropomorphite Controversy, which ascribed human characteristics to God, and ultimately denied the personhood of the Holy Spirit. This controversy recurred later in the tenth century. Augustine (354–430 AD) responded to the early controversy with his *De Trinate*, a defense of the Trinity. The Council of Chalcedon (451 AD) confirmed in Rome, Constantinople, Antioch, and Jerusalem the conclusions established in the Nicene Creed. The Synod of Toledo (589 AD) added the *filioque*[107] phrase to the Constantinople Creed, to emphasize that Holy Spirit was sent not only from the Father, but also from the Son.

Abelard (1079–1142) spoke of the Trinity in modalistic terms, referring to the names of the Father as power, the Son as wisdom, and the Spirit as goodness. Thomas Aquinas (1225–1274) further developed

---

[106] Charles Ryrie, *A Survey of Bible Doctrine* (Chicago, IL: Moody Press, 1972), 61.
[107] Latin, meaning: *and the son.*

systematic theology, countering Abelard and others, and defending Augustine's views on the Holy Spirit. But it was the Reformation (1517) that brought a more fully developed doctrine of the Holy Spirit, as Luther emphasized His role in justification by faith, Calvin emphasized His role in the Trinity and His teaching ministry. Various confessions and creeds of this era all recognized the deity of the Holy Spirit.

Still there was disagreement. Socinus (1539–1604) went even further in denying the trinity than did Arius, in that he denied the pre-existence of Christ and referred to the Holy Spirit as simply virtue and energy from God. Similarly, Arminius (1560–1609), as a direct result of his emphasis on man's autonomy, replaced the role of the Spirit with the workings of man's own volition. The Synod of Dort (1618–1619) dealt with Arminian theology as a whole and emphasized the role of the Holy Spirit in contrast to man's volition.

In the seventeenth century, John Owen (1618–1683) wrote his famous *Discourse Concerning the Holy Spirit*, a major contribution to the doctrine of the Holy Spirit. Not long afterward, Friedrich Schleiermacher (1768–1834), commonly recognized as the father of modern religious liberalism, formulated his doctrine that the trinity was modalistic, and he denied the personhood of the Spirit. The Plymouth Brethren (1825) developed an early form of Pentecostalism, which emphasized the experience of believers, taught the baptism of the Spirit as coming after salvation, and emphasized the Spirit's power and presence as central for the experience of the church.

Abraham Kuyper (1837–1920) wrote *The Work of the Holy Spirit*, acknowledging the deity and personhood of the Holy Spirit. Karl Barth (1886–1968), the recognized father of neoorthodoxy, had a modalistic approach. While he acknowledged the deity of the Spirit, Barth denied His personhood, suggesting the doctrine would lead to tritheism. Most neoorthodox theologians took Barth's doctrines a step further, denying both the deity and personality of the Holy Spirit. Neoliberalism (1900's) was a philosophy that denied most Biblical views, denying the deity of Christ, and suggesting that the Holy Spirit was simply an expression of a God whose existence was uncertain.

Modern Pentecostalism, seeking to remedy the lifelessness of the modern church, emphasized baptism of the Spirit as a second work of grace, as well as the ongoing existence of foundational gifts (in contrast to the view that those gifts had ceased in the early church). While modern Pentecostalism acknowledges the deity and personhood of the Spirit, it presented a different view of the work He does in this contemporary era.

C. Peter Wagner described the modern Pentecostal movement as coming in three waves.[108] The first was in the early 1900's with the teaching of Charles Parham and Asuza Street Revival (1906–1915), led by William Seymour. The second was the Charismatic movement of the 1960's, in which ideas like word of faith and prosperity theology spread to churches that had been previously uninfluenced by the Pentecostal movement.

---

[108] C. Peter Wagner, *The Third Wave of the Holy Spirit* (Ann Arbor, MI: Servant Publications, 1988).

The third wave began in the 1980's, centered in the Vineyard Church, with an added emphasis on signs and wonders resulting from the work of the Holy Spirit. Notable teachers in this third wave included especially Charles Wimber and C. Peter Wagner, along with others who emphasized a renewed prophetic and apostolic ministry in the church.

Stemming from these historic controversies is the contemporary debate regarding what is the present ministry of the Holy Spirit. Questions regarding His baptism and His giftings persist. At present there are three major views within the Christian church: cessationist, noncessationist, and open but cautious. Cessationism is the idea that the foundational gifts of the Holy Spirit have ceased at some point during the time of the early church. Noncessationism is the idea that all gifts, including the foundational ones, are operative in the church today. The open but cautious view is a bit more agnostic than either of the other approaches, but tends toward noncessationism.

The pages that follow are written to help believers walk through the Biblical perspectives on these issues, so that readers can have confidence that there is an answer, and that the Bible offers clarity and specificity even on some of the most difficult questions. The Holy Spirit is not a confusing person. On the contrary, He reveals and clarifies. Likewise, His word is not recorded in order to confuse believers, but rather to inform and encourage.

Wherever there might be confusion, it is usually the result of us reading our own ideas into the Biblical text, rather than simply allowing it to say what it says and allowing it to shape our ideas. The topic of the Holy Spirit and His ministry to believers is such an important piece of the Christian life. We cannot afford to be ignorant or misinformed. History shows us that where there are differences of opinion on theological matters there are usually different ways of understanding what the Bible says. The pages that follow are rooted in a natural approach to understanding the Bible,[109] and the conclusions are drawn from reading the Bible that way, and not with any pre-intention of validating one view or the other.

---

[109] Specifically, the literal grammatical-historical hermeneutic method.

28   Gifted

6
The Baptism of the Holy Spirit

The great Inigo Montoya once famously said, *"You keep using that word. I do not think it means what you think it means."*[110] That line is apropos for many occasions, but it especially fits how we often understand spiritual gifts. Instead of recognizing spiritual gifts as tools God gives to help us get His work done, we often consider them to be mystical links between God and us – evidences or proofs, if you will, that He is really working. I suppose we shouldn't be too surprised, after all we are in good company (recall Israel's episode with the golden calf – their faith was pretty weak at the time too). But still, like Montoya says, we use the words without really understanding how *He uses the words*. Consequently, we make them into something they aren't. In the next few chapters we take a look at some common myths regarding spiritual gifts. The first myth we examine is the assertion that we need a second work of grace in order to get a spiritual gift.

The Bible is notably silent about receiving the Holy Spirit as a step separate from salvation – except in the book of Acts (more on that book in a moment). Romans

---

[110] *The Princess Bride.* Directed by Rob Reiner. 20th Century Fox, 1987.

8:9, for example, says, "...But if anyone does not have the Spirit of Christ, he does not belong to Him." We either have the Spirit or we don't. We are either in Christ or we aren't. Paul leaves no middle ground. In fact, Ephesians 1:13 tells us how and when we receive the Holy Spirit: "In Him, you also, after listening to the message of truth, the gospel of your salvation – *having also believed you were sealed in Him with the Holy Spirit of promise.*" Paul adds that the Spirit is "given as a pledge [or downpayment] of our inheritance [eternal life], with a view to the redemption of God's own possession, to the praise of His glory."[111] At the moment of belief, the Holy Spirit is given to believers.

John also observes that, "By this we know that we abide in Him and He in us because He has given us of His Spirit."[112] In other words, one of the ways we can be assured of our position in Him is that He has given us His Spirit. I wonder if we realize that when we assert people don't have His Spirit because they haven't undergone some ritual, we are denying their means of assurance of salvation. The Holy Spirit is Himself a gift, and He is that for all those who have believed in Christ. *But what about baptism of the Holy Spirit?*

John announced that Jesus would baptize people with the Holy Spirit.[113] Jesus later told His disciples to make more disciples, baptizing them in the name of the Father, Son, and Holy Spirit.[114] Later still, Paul says,

---

[111] Eph 1:14.
[112] 1 Jn 4:13.
[113] Mt 3:11.
[114] Mt 28:19.

"For by one Spirit we were all baptized into one body, whether Jews of Greeks, whether slaves or free, and we were all made to drink of one Spirit."[115] Paul is describing the process where every believer becomes a part of the body of Christ.

If one has not been baptized by the Holy Spirit, he or she is not a part of the body of Christ, and is not a member of the church. If we misunderstand the baptism of the Spirit, we can kick a lot of people out of the church (in a manner of speaking) without realizing it. In short, Spirit baptism is a positional thing God does for every one of us. It is not a ritual we need to perform. Water baptism is different.

The word baptism, from the Greek *baptizo*, means to *immerse*. In water baptism, the person is immersed as a symbol of participation with Christ's death, burial, and resurrection. In Spirit baptism, the believer is immersed in the Holy Spirit, making that person a member of the body of Christ. By the way, Peter reminds us that water baptism doesn't save but the spiritual work of baptism God accomplishes in us does.[116]

But what about the book of Acts? Each of the epistles quoted so far in this chapter were written between 54-68 AD. But the church was born in about 33 AD. The book of Acts covers the history of the young church from 33-63 AD, but most of the book, from chapters 1-19, take place before 54 AD. There was a period of overlap between people who already had believed in the Messiah even before His death and

---

[115] 1 Cor 12:13.
[116] 1 Pet 3:21.

resurrection, and before the specifics of the Holy Spirit were taught, and people who had a more complete message of who the Holy Spirit was and what He did in the lives of believers.

For example, Apollos was a tremendous believer, mighty in the Scriptures. He knew Jesus and was teaching accurately about Him, but wasn't familiar with much beyond the baptism of John.[117] At Ephesus Paul found some people in the same situation – they hadn't even "heard whether there is a Holy Spirit."[118] Paul laid hands on them, and they received the Holy Spirit.[119]

When considering episodes like these in the book of Acts, it is important to remember that Acts is descriptive rather than prescriptive. It provides a historical account of what happened, not a theological description of what we should do. Of course, we can draw secondary applications from Acts, but we should be very careful not to place ourselves back into the context of the times of the book of Acts.

Acts is transitional, and if we fail to see that, we will be confused about what God is doing with the church. We live now, not then. Apollos and the other believers like him probably had believed in the Messiah before His death and resurrection. But as the church age began, they needed to be brought into that body. In their case, Paul facilitated that. Believers in the present age have no such need, because they have believed during the church age.

---

[117] Acts 18:24-25.
[118] Acts 19:2.
[119] Acts 19:6.

According to Paul, John, and Peter, in this age, those in Christ *have* the Spirit, and are already part of the body of Christ. In short, there is no such thing, Biblically speaking, as a "second work of grace" for believers today. Nor is there any need (or possibility) for us to do what God has already done for us. The Holy Spirit is in every believer, and He gives to us what we need for His service. He has baptized all of us, and He indwells all of us.

7

The Role of the Holy Spirit In Our Understanding of Scripture

The theological term most commonly used by theologians to express the role of the Holy Spirit in Biblical understanding is *illumination*. While the term isn't directly used of the Holy Spirit, the concept is present, for example in John 1:5 and 1:9, "The Light shines in the darkness, and the darkness did not comprehend it...the true Light which coming into the world, enlightens every man." In this context Jesus is the Light, and His enlightening or illumining work is accomplished with everyone.

But if Christ illumines everyone, to what extent does the Holy Spirit illumine? Does the Bible even teach that the Holy Spirit illumines, or is illumination by the Holy Spirit a theological rather than exegetical concept?

There are essentially three distinct views regarding the role of the Holy Spirit in interpretation, including: (1) the idea that "the Holy Spirit brings to the Christian greater cognitive understanding" of the Bible,[120] (2) the idea that "one of the unique roles of the Holy Spirit

---

[120] Robert Plummer, *40 Questions About Interpreting the Bible* (Grand Rapids, MI: Kregel, 2010), 144.

is to convict, convince, and arouse sluggish hearts by applying the truths perceived in the text of Scripture to the lives of individuals,"[121] and (3) the idea that "the basic thrust of the Holy Spirit's illuminating or enlightening work relates primarily to our welcoming of the truths rather than our understanding of them."[122]

Simply put, the views are that the Holy Spirit helps in cognitive understanding, the Holy Spirit helps with application, or the Holy Spirit helps a person receive rather than understand the truths of Scripture. To keep things simple, this discussion will refer to (1) the cognitive view, (2) the application view, and (3) the reception view. Let's examine the Biblical data to determine which of these views, if any – or more than one – best represents what the Bible teaches.

We start with the Psalms, a book that makes clear that God indeed illumines. Psalm 18:28 reads, "For You light my lamp; The Lord my God illumines my darkness." Psalm 19:8 adds that "The commandment of the Lord is pure, enlightening the eyes." Psalm 119, which includes a reference to Scripture in virtually all of its 176 verses, gives some insight regarding the concept of illumination. Psalm 119:18 records the Psalmist's request –perhaps for illumination: "Open my eyes, that I may behold wonderful things from Your law." The Psalmist later seems to acknowledge how the eyes are actually opened: "Your

---

[121] William Craig, Craig Blomberg, and Robert Hubbard Jr., *Introduction to Biblical Introduction, Revised and Updated* (Nashville, TN: Thomas Nelson, 2004), 139.
[122] Walt Russell, Playing With Fire (Carol Stream, IL: Navpress, 2000), 63.

word is a lamp to my feet, and a light to my path."[123] This latter passage is particularly helpful because it identifies how God illumines, or specifically through what vehicle He illumines. It is the word of God that is the lamp to the Psalmist's feet, in this particular context. The Psalmist adds for good measure, "The unfolding of Your words gives light; it gives understanding to the simple." Again, it is the word that illumines. Consequently, none of the three views are addressed in these Psalms, nor is the Holy Spirit directly mentioned at all in these contexts. So we reserve judgment for further examination, armed with the simple knowledge from the Psalms passages that God illumines, and He does it through His word.

In John 14:26, Jesus encourages his eleven disciples, saying to them, "But the Helper, the Holy Spirit, whom the Father will send in My name, He will teach you all things, and bring to your remembrance all that I said to you." The Holy Spirit will teach them all things. Jesus adds in John 16:13 that the Spirit of truth will guide them into "all the truth," including disclosing to them "what is to come." These are vitally important passages to put in proper context. Jesus is addressing eleven men, assuring them of the Holy Spirit's ministry *to them*. There is no exegetical reason to suggest that the ministry of guiding into all the truth extends beyond this prophecy that Peter recognizes is fulfilled in the recording of Scripture (see 2 Pet 1:20-21). Once again, these passages do not speak to any of the three views on illumination. Instead these encouraging prophesies from

---

[123] Ps 119:105.

Jesus help prepare the eleven for the challenging task they would face when Jesus would depart.

In Luke 24:45 we encounter Jesus opening the minds of the disciples to understand the Scriptures, and specifically the Law, the Prophets, and the Psalms – the three basic divisions of the Hebrew Bible. The passage doesn't give explanation regarding how He opened their minds, but it appears He did so by explaining, as He appeals to Scripture and explains them in the verses that immediately follow.[124] He concludes the discourse with a prophecy of power that would come to his listeners – a prophecy corresponding to the promise of the Holy Spirit made in the upper room.[125] This passage is descriptive of an event that happened, but doesn't provide any data that would lead one to conclude the event (that Jesus somehow opened the minds to cognitively understand Scripture) is normative in the life of the believer. While the passage does provide an instance of cognitive illumination, the Holy Spirit is not identified as having a direct part in it (in fact, He hadn't even been sent by Father and Son yet), nor does the passage specifically identify how Jesus accomplished this opening of their minds (though the implication is that He did so by explaining). Once again, we cannot conclude in favor of any of the three views based on this passage.

Romans 8:9 is clear in its assertion that if a person does not have the Spirit of Christ – the Spirit of God dwelling in him – then that person does not belong to God. Paul adds a few verses later that "all who are being

---

[124] Lk 24:46-48.
[125] Jn 14:26, 16:13.

led by the Spirit of God, these are sons of God."[126] Further, Paul explains, "the Spirit Himself testifies with our spirit that we are children of God."[127] Clearly, by this point in the early history of the church, the Holy Spirit was the grounding of every believer's life in Christ. Ephesians 1:13-14 discusses how the Holy Spirit is even the guarantee or down payment of eternal life. In these Romans verses, Paul identifies the Spirit as indwelling,[128] leading,[129] and testifying.[130] With respect to the indwelling and testifying, there is no action implied on the part of the believer. But with respect to His leading, it is implied that the believer is following. The question in view here is how the Holy Spirit leads, and whether or not that is connected to the concept of illumination.

Four times in the New Testament the Spirit is mentioned as *leading*. Matthew and Luke describe the Spirit leading Jesus into and in the wilderness to be tempted by Satan,[131] and Paul twice refers to the Spirit's leading – once in Romans 8:14, asserting that all who are being led (present, passive) by the Spirit of God are sons of God, and in a similar context in Galatians 5:18, if believers are being led (present, passive) by the Spirit, then they are not under law. Both of Paul's references to the Spirit's leading are present tense and passive from the believer's perspective – meaning that the leading is

---

[126] Rom 8:14.
[127] Rom 8:16.
[128] Rom 8:9, 11.
[129] Rom 8:11.
[130] Rom 8:16.
[131] Mt 4:1, Lk 4:1.

ongoing, and that the Spirit is the one doing the action, and the believer is simply responding.

In these contexts the leading of the Spirit isn't explicitly explained, but Galatians 5:25 gives us a hint of what that leading looks like: if we are living by the Spirit, then we should be walking in Him. There is a connection between His leading and our walking in Him. Simply put, if we are being led by Him, we are walking with Him. But still, nothing in these immediate contexts are indicative of a connection to illumination.

Another term we encounter that is related to knowledge is the anointing believers have from the Holy One that results in "you all know"[132] or "you know all things."[133] In the immediately following context, that knowledge is the knowledge of the truth.[134] This passage does not identify what the anointing or assignment is, so it would be difficult to support this passage as a proof text for the illuminating work of the Holy Spirit. Yet, in at least two separate contexts in 1 John, the Spirit is directly bringing about knowledge for the believer: in 3:24 we know He abides in us through the Spirit, and in 4:13 we know that we abide in Him, because He has given of His Spirit. Both of these assurances are accomplished simply by the truth of His presence. Once again, no illuminating work is directly in view. However, 1 John 2:27 describes the anointing as abiding in believers, and teaches them about all things.

---

[132] 1 Jn 2:20, NASB.
[133] 1 Jn 2:20, KJV.
[134] 1 Jn 2:21.

Besides the reference in 2:27, John uses the term abide in reference to several general relationships: (1) the believer abiding in Him,[135] (2) the word of God abiding in believers,[136] (3) God abiding in believers,[137] (4) the believer abiding in death,[138] (5) eternal life not abiding in the murderer,[139] (6) love of God abiding in believers,[140] and (7) believers abiding in His love.[141]

Of these options, it seems that the anointing of 2:27 refers to the word of God, as a neuter pronoun is used rather than masculine, and it teaches about all things. While we certainly cannot exegetically disconnect the Spirit from this anointing, we also can't *directly* connect Him in any of the three senses of illumination.

In 1 Corinthians 2:6-11 Paul describes how God revealed His wisdom through the Spirit. Verse 12 makes clear that the Spirit is a Person, and not an "it." Also, the verse indicates that we have received the Spirit of God that we may understand[142] that which has been freely given by God. In the thought that follows,[143] Paul contrasts a natural[144] man and a spiritual[145] one. The natural man does not receive[146] the things of God's Spirit

---

[135] 1 Jn 2:6, 10, 24c, 28, 3:6, 24a, 4:13, 15b.
[136] 1 Jn 2:14, 24.
[137] 1 Jn 3:9, 24b, 4:12, 15a, 16b.
[138] 1 Jn 3:14.
[139] 1 Jn 3:15.
[140] 1 Jn 3:17.
[141] 1 Jn 4:16a.
[142] Greek, *eidomen*.
[143] 1 Cor 2:14-16.
[144] Greek, *psuchikos*.
[145] Greek, *pneumatos*.
[146] Greek, *dechetai*.

— they are foolishness to the natural man, and he cannot experientially know[147] them because they can only be spiritually judged or discerned.[148] Paul chastises the Corinthians because, while they have the mind of Christ,[149] they are walking as fleshly[150] rather than spiritual.[151] In other words, they have an incredible resource at their disposal in order to know intimately or experientially, but instead they were choosing to walk in ignorant immaturity.

In this context the wisdom is available to these believers, but it is not discerned or judged rightly because it is not received by these believers as it should be. There seems no reference here to illumination, *per se*, but rather to being properly connected to what has already been provided. We have the Spirit of God, He has revealed wisdom, we have the mind of Christ. Consequently, it is an absurdity if we do not understand what God has provided. If we fail in that way, then we are being fleshly, behaving and thinking as natural rather than spiritual people.

From 1 Corinthians 2:6-3:3 we can see how the ministry of the Spirit enables believers to have a better knowledge, but that seems to extend beyond understanding[152] to more experiential or personal knowledge,[153] as indicated by the distinct terms Paul

---

[147] Greek, *gnonai*.
[148] Greek, *anakrinetai*.
[149] 1 Cor 2:16.
[150] Greek, *sarchinois*.
[151] 1 Cor 3:1ff.
[152] Greek, *oida*.
[153] Greek, *gnosis*.

The Role of the Holy Spirit in Our Understanding 43

uses. The natural man isn't receiving, because he doesn't have the Spirit, and therefore he isn't discerning or judging properly. But the cognitive understanding seems to be there. It does not appear that the Spirit is active in providing additional cognitive understanding, though clearly through Him God has revealed wisdom, which definitely results in greater cognitive understanding.[154] But that understanding is not the result of ongoing activity by the Spirit in the believer, it seems more the result of responding properly to what He has already revealed.

The cognitive model for illumination doesn't seem to fit this context, nor does the application model, as the Corinthians are chastised for not applying properly what they already had – the mind of Christ.[155] They also weren't welcoming what God had revealed – not because the Holy Spirit wasn't doing His job, but because they weren't doing theirs. Once again, none of the three popular models of illumination seems to fit Paul's instruction here.

The reference to illumining in 1 Corinthians 4:5 speaks of how the Lord will return, bringing to light that which is hidden in the darkness and the motives of hearts. The context is not of judgment unto punishment, but unto praise or reward, as each person's praise or excellence will come to him by God. The last three verbs in this verse are all future. They don't describe a present work of the Spirit, but rather a future work of the Son.

---

[154] 1 Cor 2:12.
[155] 1 Cor 2:16.

After expounding on the marvelous glory of God expressed through the work of the Father, Son, and Spirit in salvation, in Ephesians 1:17-18 Paul offers a prayer for the believers, that God would give to them "a spirit of wisdom and revelation in the knowledge of Him." He has already told believers that they have the Spirit,[156] so this prayer is not that believers would have Him, but that they would have a spirit, in the more general sense, of wisdom and unveiling in the knowledge[157] of Him. The first of these two verses is a request for greater experiential knowledge, whereas the second verse requests greater cognitive understanding[158] of the implications of what Paul had just explained in 1:1-14 and what he would expound on in chapters 2-3 – specifically, the hope and riches God has provided to believers.

Paul is praying here that believers would truly understand God's word. Unlike in his letter to the Corinthians, where Paul puts the onus on the believer, Paul seems to recognize here that the believer has some need that God can or must meet. Because the provision for that is not connected directly to the Holy Spirit in this context, it seems unwise to assume Paul is praying that the Holy Spirit might illuminate believers to understand. Even if that is what Paul was praying for, it wouldn't be normative, since Paul places the burden of understanding on believers themselves in other contexts (as in 1 Corinthians). Instead, it seems that Paul recognizes the

---

[156] Eph 1:13-14.
[157] Greek, *epignosei*.
[158] Greek, *eidenai*.

depth of "the surpassing greatness of His power to those who believe," and wishes for believers to recognize the implications of that greatness.

As Paul concludes the section on the believer's position in Christ, he offers another prayer that God would grant them "to be strengthened with power through His Spirit in the inner man,"[159] ultimately so that they will be able to comprehend or grasp[160] the breadth, length, height, and depth, and to experientially know[161] the love of Christ. In this context, Paul does connect the believers' receiving and experientially knowing with the present and ongoing ministry of the Holy Spirit. This passage would seem to support the third model of illumination, providing a welcoming, leading to better experiential knowledge. If one understands the verb *to know* (*gnonai*) as cognitive (I don't), rather than experiential, then one could easily recognize this passage as supporting the cognitive illumination view instead. Either way, it is clear from this passage that the Holy Spirit is indeed involved in the believer's processing of the truth. Whether or not that involvement is best represented by the term *illumination* is the question.

In 2 Timothy 2:7 Paul tells Timothy to think on what he says, and he adds that God will give Timothy understanding[162] in everything. The formula is this: you take action (imperative), and God will take action (future). Perhaps more than any other previous reference,

---

[159] Eph 3:16.
[160] Greek, *katalabesthai*.
[161] Greek, *gnonai*.
[162] Greek, *sunesin*.

this one shows the relationship between God and man in the process of increasing cognitive understanding. Both Timothy and God have a responsibility here. Once again, this is not tied specifically to the Holy Spirit, but we have seen previously that the Holy Spirit is certainly involved in the process.

Hebrews 6:4 references "the having been enlightened,"[163] as "having tasted" (twice), "having been made partakers," and "having fallen away." Because each verb is a participle, and only the first has the definite article, the person being described here *has participated in each of these things*. This seems a clear reference to believers who are neglecting their salvation,[164] and who cannot come to repentance as long as they continue to put Christ to open shame.[165] The enlightenment here refers to their positional change from death to life, rather than to an ongoing learning or growth process. Enlightenment accompanied tasting the heavenly gift and being made partakers of the Holy Spirit. Ongoing or continuing illumination of the Holy Spirit is not in view here.

Conclusion

From these passages, it is evident that the Holy Spirit is actively involved in the ongoing growth of the believer. It is also evident that He was actively involved in the revealing of God's truth through the Bible. It is evident from these and other contexts that He uses the Scriptures in the lives of believers, and that those

---

[163] Greek, *photisthentos*.
[164] See Heb 2:2-3.
[165] Heb 6:6.

Scriptures are the basis for the Christian's walking in the Spirit. Further it is evident that the Holy Spirit actively helps believers to understand,[166] comprehend (receive) and to know (experientially).[167] Yet it is probably best not to describe the Holy Spirit's work in that regard as *illumination*. Further, to quantify His ministry specifically as only bringing cognitive understanding, or only helping to apply, or only helping to receive, does not seem to be exegetically justified, and may go too far (or not far enough) in defining His work. It is also important to recognize that His ministry is not remedying any inherent deficiency or limitation in the text. Instead He uses the text itself to inform and to illumine us.[168]

Paul's model in Ephesians 3:14-19 is a helpful one: he relies on the text to inform us, and he prays that we too would be able to receive "with all the saints what is the breadth and length and height and depth, and to know (experientially or intimately) the love of Christ which surpasses knowledge" that we might be filled up to all the fullness of God. This involves the Father (it is His fullness we are being filled with), it involves the Son (it is His love we are knowing), and it involves the Spirit (it is His power that strengthens us). Ultimately, we are commanded to grow.[169] We grow by His word,[170] and God, Himself, causes the growth.[171]

---

[166] 2 Tim 2:7.
[167] Eph 3:16-19.
[168] Ps 119:105.
[169] 2 Pet 3:18.
[170] 1 Pet 2:2,
[171] 1 Cor 3:7.

48   Gifted

8

Do We Value God's Communication?

God has communicated to us in three ways. First, in creation itself – in nature: David describes the function of the heavens, for example, as declaring His glory.[172] Paul adds that, "since the creation of the world His invisible attributes, His eternal power and divine nature have been clearly seen, being understood through what has been made."[173]

Second, God has communicated through "men moved by the Holy Spirit [who] spoke from God,"[174] and He did so "in the prophets in many portions and in many ways."[175] These men wrote, over a period of roughly fifteen hundred years what God revealed to them, and what Paul describes in this way: "All Scripture is God-breathed and profitable for teaching, for reproof, for correction, for training in righteousness."[176]

---

[172] Ps 19:1-6.
[173] Rom 1:20.
[174] 2 Pet 1:21.
[175] Heb 1:1.
[176] 2 Tim 3:16.

The third way God has communicated to us is in His Son,[177] who has uniquely explained the Father.[178] Those who were with Jesus during His earthly ministry and heard Him speak were receiving real-time revelation from God, but even still Jesus constantly directed His hearers back to the written word. When facing the temptations of Satan, Jesus responded, "It is written."[179] When announcing His own messianic ministry, He read from Isaiah 61:1-2a.[180] Further, He explained that He was Himself a central theme of the Scriptures.[181] In other words, even those who heard Him teach were reminded that His teaching was rooted in God's written revelation. For us today, we can only know of Jesus through what has been written. Consequently, God's written word holds great value for us, and should be treasured (though not worshipped, of course, because it is the means, not the end, but it is His means of allowing us to know Him).

David proclaims the value of God's word, as "perfect, restoring the soul...sure, making wise the simple...right, rejoicing the heart...pure, enlightening the eyes...clean, enduring forever...and true, and righteous altogether."[182] David adds that it is more desirable than refined gold and sweeter than the best honey.[183] Further, it warns its readers and offers great reward.[184] Paul

---

[177] Heb 1:1.
[178] Jn 1:18.
[179] Mt 4:4, 7, 10.
[180] Lk 4:17-21.
[181] Jn 5:39.
[182] Ps 19:7-9.
[183] Ps 19:10.
[184] Ps 19:11.

likewise recognizes the lofty value of God's written word as, "profitable for teaching, for reproof, for correction, for training in righteousness."[185] He also tells us the purpose for which God's word was committed to writing: "so that the man of God may be adequate, equipped for every good work."[186]

In His word, God has given us everything we need in order to know how to know Him.[187] In those pages He has told us much about Himself, allowing us to increase in our knowledge of and intimacy with Him.[188] And in His word He has provided for us all that we need for our daily walk with Him – including our continual, moment-by-moment growth and service. So how could we not value His word above wealth and pleasures (i.e., gold and honey)? What might capture our gaze so that we give little or no attention to that which offers the greatest of rewards? What deceptions might draw us away from His majesty and splendor, revealed in writing? When our priorities don't include the greatest of treasures, then we need to reset our priorities. Instead of settling for mere gold and honey, let's cherish something far greater.

---

[185] 2 Tim 3:16.
[186] 2 Tim 3:17.
[187] E.g., Jn 3:16.
[188] Jn 17:3.

9

Five Introductory Concepts For Understanding Spiritual Gifts

How do we figure out what spiritual gift we have? How do we use it? What is it for? What if it doesn't seem like we have any spiritual gifts? Do we have more than one? There are lots of worthy questions about spiritual gifts, and it is very helpful that the Biblical answers are straightforward. Three passages are especially helpful in discussing gifts: 1 Corinthians 12, Romans 12, and 1 Peter 4. From these passages, with help from a few others, we can glean at least five important concepts for understanding spiritual gifts.

1. What is a Spiritual Gift?

There are varieties of gifts, ministries, and effects,[189] "but to each one is given the manifestation of the Spirit for the common good.[190] In this context the definition is simply the manifestation of the Spirit. In Peter's explanation,[191] he uses the Greek *charisma*, meaning *grace gift*, to describe the same thing. These are

---

[189] 1 Cor 12:4-6.
[190] 1 Cor 12:4-7.
[191] 1 Pet 4:10.

given to believers by God to do the work of His Spirit. In other words, the design is that when the Spirit of God is working in the body of Christ, often times it is through people.

2. What Is The Purpose of Spiritual Gifts?

Very simply put, gifts are given for the common good.[192] They are said to be given by the Holy Spirit to individuals, according His own will[193] for the good of the body. We are individual members, but together we make up the body of Christ.[194] Paul compares our individual functions as members of the body of Christ to human anatomy: the body has eyes, hands, head, feet. All parts are important and work together for the good of the body.[195] While some gifts were temporary[196] and others endure, all gifts are important for the growth of the body, and ultimately for His glory.

Peter reminds us to use gifts in serving one another[197] and for the ultimate purpose of glorifying God.[198] We misuse His gifts if we don't use them for His prescribed purpose, and that purpose is clear – serving one another that God might be glorified.

---

[192] 1 Cor 12:7.
[193] Rom 12:10.
[194] Rom 12:27.
[195] Rom: 12:18-27.
[196] E.g., tongues, healing, and prophecy (1 Cor 13:8-10, Heb 2:4).
[197] 1 Pet 4:10.
[198] 1 Pet 4:11.

3. Opportunity or Ability?

Romans 12:6 notes, "we have gifts that differ according to the grace given to us." The list of gifts in 12:6-8 is very interesting, because it includes things like service, exhorting, and mercy. Obviously, it is important to recognize that our ability to have mercy, for example, is a gift from God. Without His mercy, we can't have mercy on others. Still, mercy is something that all believers should show.[199] So why is it described as a grace-gift?

Spiritual gifts seem to be more about opportunity than ability. If we have opportunity to show mercy it is because God has provided opportunity to do so. If we have opportunity to exhort or to serve – those opportunities come from God. The Bible teaches every believer how to serve, exhort, and show mercy. But just because we learn well and are prepared doesn't mean we will have opportunity to put those things into practice. Opportunities are just as important as abilities, and both come from God.[200]

4. Given or Developed?

So which is it? Are these gifts simply given or do we have a responsibility to develop them? The answer is yes to both. In everything we do we should be growing.[201] For example, we may be gifted as a teacher[202] – provided either opportunity, ability or both – but there is still a responsibility to learn that which we are supposed to

---

[199] Jam 2:13, Jude 22-23.
[200] Eph 2:10.
[201] 1 Thes 4:1, 10, 2 Pet 3:18.
[202] Rom 12:7.

teach.[203] If God provides us the opportunity to teach, and we haven't spent the time and effort to prepare, then we aren't going to be of much good to others.

5. How To Know What Gift(s) We Have Been Given?

To answer this question some go to great lengths – even employing personality tests to determine what one's spiritual gift is. But the Biblical approach is so much simpler than all that. Galatians 6:10 encourages us this way: "while we have opportunity, let us do good to all people, and especially to those who are of the household of faith." *While we have opportunity.* Do you have opportunity to serve? Then serve. Do you have opportunity to show mercy? To help? To teach? To lead? Then do those things.

The Bible never encourages us to try to figure out what gift or gifts we may have (nor does it prohibit that, of course). Instead, we are to be equipped by His word for every good work.[204] The opportunity to do those works is prepared beforehand.[205] Actually, we might not ever know what our spiritual gifts were until we look back on a lifetime of ministry. Did God use you as a teacher? Or a leader? Or a servant? Or an exhorter? Then it would seem that God gifted you in those areas. Of course, it is perfectly fine to prefer to serve God in particular ways. He tells us to delight ourselves in Him and He will give us the desire of our hearts.[206] But we must always be

---

[203] 2 Tim 2:2.
[204] 2 Tim 3:16-17.
[205] Eph 2:10.
[206] Ps 37:3.

available to Him for whatever task He desires us to do, and we must be prepared to take advantage of any opportunity.

Here's another way to look at it. If a believer is being used in the body of Christ as a teacher, and that believer sees a person who needs mercy, should that believer show mercy or not? How about this: "Honey, I have the gift of exhorting, but I don't have the gift of service, so I can't help you with the cleaning – but I can encourage and exhort you while you do the cleaning." We need to stop looking for divine excuses to avoid tasks we don't prefer, and we need to start presenting our bodies a living and holy sacrifice to Him.[207] What has He put in front of us to do? Then we need to do that. He has given us the opportunity and the ability. Let's not waste either, and let's be prepared for both.

---

[207] Rom 12:1-2.

58   Gifted

10

Does Every Believer Have a Spiritual Gift?

The phrase *spiritual gift* is only employed five times in the NASB New Testament. In Romans 1:11[208] it is in reference to something Paul wanted to impart to the entire church at Rome. In 1 Corinthians 12:1, Paul prefaces the entire discussion of manifestations of the Spirit with the expressed desire that the Corinthians be aware of spiritual gifts, but while the Greek includes the term *spiritual*,[209] it does not include any term for *gifts*, thus, while the NASB reading implies that the context following verse 1 is a discussion of spiritual gifts, the Greek does not necessarily support that implication.

In 1 Corinthians 14:1 and 12 likewise, the NASB includes the phrase *spiritual gifts,* but the Greek only includes the term *spiritual*[210] and no term from which the NASB translates *gifts*. Finally, in 1 Timothy 4:14 Paul warns Timothy not to neglect the spiritual gift within him. In light of the small number of references in the NASB – only five, and the even smaller number of actual

---

[208] Greek, *charisma humin pneumatikon.*
[209] Greek, *pneumatikon.*
[210] Greek, *pneumatika, pneumaton.*

references in the Greek – two, there is no Biblical data to support the idea that every believer has something specifically referred to as a *spiritual gift*. On the other hand, there is data supporting every believer's having a manifestation of the Spirit for the common good.[211]

1 Corinthians 12:4-7 describes the manifestation[212] of the Holy Spirit given to each believer, in three different forms: gifts,[213] ministries,[214] and effects.[215] There is a diversity of forms given within and to the body, and not every member of the body is necessarily given all three forms. In this context, there is no explicit statement that every believer is given a spiritual gift, but rather simply the manifestation of the Spirit for the common good.[216] How that manifestation is dispersed is determined by the will of the Spirit.

Some are given gifts, while others are given ministries or services, while still others are given effects or activities. Paul makes no effort to comprehensively categorize the specific examples mentioned in verses 8-10, though he does categorize two: gifts of healing[217] and effecting of miracles.[218] The remainder of the list remains uncategorized: prophecy, distinguishing of spirits, tongues, and interpretation of tongues. It is evident that Paul's intent is not a precise catalogue of the Spirit's

---

[211] 1 Cor 12:7.
[212] Greek, *phanerosis*.
[213] Greek, *charismaton*, in 1 Cor 12:4.
[214] Greek, *diakonion*, in 1 Cor 12:5.
[215] Greek, *energematon*, in 1 Cor 12:6.
[216] 1 Cor 12:7.
[217] 1 Cor 12:9, 28, 30.
[218] 1 Cor 12:10.

manifestations and their categories. Instead, Paul's emphasis is the common Source (the Holy Spirit) and purpose (the common good) of these manifestations.

Romans 12:6-8 describes that we are *having* gifts according to the grace given us. While again Paul doesn't reference each example specifically as a gift, the implication is that they are each gifts: prophecy, service,[219] teaching, exhorting, giving, leading, and mercy. Two things should be noted here. First, Paul does not reference these as spiritual gifts at all. The Greek term *charismata* simply references a gift of grace. To categorize these all as spiritual gifts isn't warranted in this context from Paul's verbiage. Second, at least aspects of teaching,[220] exhorting,[221] and giving[222] are the common expectation of all believers, not just those who have particular gifts.

1 Peter 4:10-11 notes that "each one has received a gift,"[223] and provides only two examples: speaking and serving. Either he is identifying two categories of gifts – those that involve speaking and those that involve serving – or he is citing two specific gifts as examples, both of which functions seem to be common expectations of believers.[224]

---

[219] Greek, *diakonian*, the same word translated by the NASB as *ministries* in 1 Cor 12:5
[220] Col 3:16.
[221] 1 Thes 5:11.
[222] 2 Cor 9:6-8.
[223] Greek, *charisma*.
[224] See Eph 5:19 and Gal 5:13, though the Greek *douleuete* is used here rather than *diakoneo*, as is used in 1 Pet 4:10-11.

Though there is no explicit claim that every believer has a spiritual gift, there is clear evidence that every believer has a manifestation of the Holy Spirit, and that manifestation can take a number of forms. Certainly, believers have gifts from God, and if one wanted to call those gifts *spiritual gifts*, since they are all connected to the Holy Spirit, that doesn't seem too problematic – as long as we handle the Biblical terminology with precision. But practically speaking, there is much data given regarding the source of the manifestations and gifts, and regarding the purpose. So rather than focus, to the point of paralysis, on identifying exactly how the Spirit is manifesting in our lives, we should simply be submitted to Him and eager to meet whatever opportunity He provides us to be of benefit to the body.

Do I have any *spiritual gifts*? I have absolutely no idea, and am not even a bit concerned about that uncertainty. I am, on the other hand certain of the Spirit's manifesting Himself in our lives for the good of those in Christ. If we are allowing His word to dwell richly in us, we can be confident that He will grant us whatever enablement is needed to meet the opportunity of the moment, for His glory. He tells us that much, even if He doesn't tell us every detail of how He accomplishes that in us.

11

Identifying Spiritual Gifts

He had no military training, and no skill with the elite weapons of war, but when he saw a battle that needed to be won he didn't hesitate to engage. Against all odds, and armed only with the knowledge of how God had strengthened him before, a sling and a few small stones, David faced a vicious enemy. 1 Samuel 17 gives the account of how David heard the Philistines taunting God and the armies of Israel, how no soldiers were willing to fight the Philistine champion, and how David – depending on the Lord – won the day.

Being only a boy, David was met with resistance when he volunteered to fight. King Saul told him he was not able.[225] David's response was brilliant (and helpful): "The Lord who delivered me from the paw of the lion and from the paw of the bear, He will deliver me from the hand of this Philistine."[226] And of course, we know the rest of the story.

David's attitude toward serving God provides an excellent example for us today, especially as we consider spiritual gifts. David lived in a different age, and the Holy Spirit was not operating in exactly the same way – He

---

[225] 1 Sam 17:33.
[226] 1 Sam 17:37.

would temporarily strengthen people for specific tasks, and there is no evidence that He indwelt people then as He does in the church age. Because David wasn't dealing with "spiritual gifts," I use his episode with Goliath as an example, but we have to be careful not to take the analogy too far.

In any case, David was certain he would be able to function successfully in a future endeavor only because of how God provided for him in similar past endeavors. He exhibited no fear in looking forward to the task at hand because of his history with God. But as far as we know, David had no special revelation from God to that point. As far as the Bible reveals, God did not promise David He would deliver him from the lion or the bear – or Goliath. But yet David was confident, and he proclaimed to Goliath, "I come to you in the name of the Lord of hosts, the God of the armies of Israel, whom you have taunted."[227]

Let's fast-forward now three thousand years. We know that church-age believers are given spiritual gifts.[228] But there is something very odd about these gifts. Nowhere in the Bible is there any indication of specifically how we can know what gift(s) we have been given. All we are told is how the gifts are to be employed – for the common good,[229] and in serving one another as good stewards of the manifold grace of God.[230] There is simply no data about how we are to identify our spiritual

---

[227] 1 Sam 17:45.
[228] Rom 12:6, 1 Cor 12:4ff, 1 Pet 4:10.
[229] 1 Cor 12:7.
[230] 1 Pet 4:10.

gifts. So where does that leave us? We know He gives gifts, and we know we receive them, but we have no way of being certain what gift He has given.

First we must consider that the equipping for good works never comes from spiritual gifts, it comes from the word of God.[231] If we neglect His word, we simply will not be equipped for His service, for we will not understand how He has designed His gifts to be used and why. Second, we need to recognize that "There are varieties of ministries, and the same Lord. There are varieties of effects, but the same God who works all things in all."[232] God has created different gifts and ministries and is capable of using them all however He wishes in order to achieve the result He desires. If we are allowing His word to dwell richly in us,[233] then we know we are being equipped for whatever task He has for us, because, "All Scripture is God-breathed and profitable for teaching, for reproof, for correction, for training in righteousness; so that the man of God may be adequate, equipped for every good work."[234] Paul adds, "Whatever you do in word or deed, do all in the name of the Lord Jesus, giving thanks through Him to God the Father."[235] Just as David opposed Goliath in the name of the Lord, in that same way we should encounter all our own activities.

Further, David was able to have confidence in God's future dealings because of His past performance. I

---

[231] 2 Tim 3:16-17.
[232] 1 Cor 12:5-6.
[233] Col 3:16.
[234] 2 Tim 3:16-17.
[235] Col 3:17.

suggest that spiritual gifts work the same way. While we have absolutely no way of quantifying what our spiritual gift(s) may be, we can look at how God has used us in the past, giving us particular opportunities and helping us make the most of them. Consequently, we can have confidence in the future that whenever He has a task for us, He has already provided for our equipping through His word (which we must allow to abide in us), that we are as spiritually gifted as He needs us to be in order to engage the task, and that, ultimately, success from His perspective is not brought about by skill and superiority from our perspective.

So we can focus less on trying to identify how He has gifted us, and avoid the paralysis that comes from the predictable uncertainty about our gifts. He simply hasn't told us and offers no mechanism for us to discern such gifts. Instead we are exhorted to do all that we do in the name of Christ – meaning, as if we were representing Him in that activity. If we are thinking, speaking, and working as Christ would, then we know we are on the right track. And rather than looking forward to predict specifically how God might use us, we can prepare diligently and make the most of every opportunity He provides.

When people ask me what spiritual gift(s) God has given me, I tell them I have absolutely no idea – I just try to be faithful with every moment, and seek to accomplish whatever He puts in front of me to accomplish. I am certain of His provision, but beyond what He has revealed I have no need of certainty about how He intends to use me. Some things we can't know, and other things we can.

We can know, like David, that whatever we may encounter in the future, God has provided the means for our equipping. Perhaps we can look back one day on a lifetime of service to Him, and discover that He used us repeatedly in particular ways. Perhaps looking back we will be able to see more clearly how He gifted us. But in the meantime, let's look forward with our eyes focused on Him.[236] We can't go wrong if we are following Him.

---

[236] Heb 12:2.

12

I Can't Help...
I Don't Have That Gift

Romans 12:6-8 describes eight gifts: prophecy, serving, teaching, exhorting, giving, leading, and mercy. 1 Corinthians 12:8-10 lists nine manifestations of the Spirit: word of wisdom, word of knowledge, faith, gifts of healing, miracles, prophecy, distinguishing of spirits, tongues, interpretation of tongues. Verse 28 adds eight appointments: apostles, prophets, teachers, miracles, healings, helps, administrations, and tongues. 1 Peter 4:11 mentions two gifts: speaking and serving.

We know that every believer has the Spirit of God,[237] that "we have gifts that differ,"[238] that to "each one is given a manifestation of the Spirit,"[239] and that "each one has received a special gift."[240] We also know that while identifying one's spiritual gifts(s) with certainty is not required and may not even be entirely possible, the Spirit's giving and manifesting is not at all irrelevant. These gifts are designed to play an important role in the church.

---
[237] Rom 8:9, Eph 1:13-14.
[238] Rom 12:6.
[239] 1 Cor 12:7.
[240] 1 Pet 4:10.

After all, they are deliberately tasked *means* designed to work toward one vital *end*: "so that in all things God may be glorified through Jesus Christ, to whom belongs the glory and dominion forever and ever. Amen."[241] If their purpose is His glory, then ignoring them is not an option.

But if a person is, for example, fairly certain that they have been gifted with teaching, then what are they to do when faced with a different ministry opportunity having little or nothing to do with teaching? What if there is a financial need in the church that the "teacher" is aware of and has the means to help resolve. Can he claim that he is *only* to function as a teacher, and hasn't got the gift of helps? Does this absolve him of any responsibility toward the needy family?

2 Corinthians 8:14 describes the purpose of abundance as for supplying needs (without any reference to spiritual gifting, by the way). Paul adds in 9:8 a broader purpose statement for abundance: "...always having all sufficiency in everything, you may have an abundance *for every good deed.*" *Every good deed* implies that one's work and service is to extend beyond personal spiritual gifting, though a case could be made that all gifting – including God's provision of material wealth – is spiritual gifting.

Consider that in 1 Timothy 3:2, Paul requires that an overseer should be above reproach. If an overseer perceived himself as gifted only as a teacher or a leader, and was unwilling to push a mop or lend a helping hand

---

[241] 1 Pet 4:11b.

where needed, I doubt he could ever be considered above reproach – in fact, he would likely encounter quite a bit of reproach. Further, one could question whether that overseer could be an effective teacher or leader without a readiness to help, to serve, to administer. Evidently, there is interplay among the gifts, and that shouldn't at all be surprising. After all, they work together for the same purpose: His glory.

If the goal is His glory, then at every opportunity we should be ready to step in and use whatever resources He has given in order to meet the need of the moment. Remember Paul's example in 1 Corinthians 9:22-23: "...I have become all things to all men, so that I may by all means save some." If Paul was willing to do whatever was needed in his evangelistic efforts, then what about us in our efforts to serve in the body? Are we entirely available for God's use, or will we only answer the call when particular needs arise? Have we become so introspective that we are crippled for all but the narrowest of tasks? That paralysis wouldn't seem compatible with "adequate, equipped for every good work,"[242] would it?

---

[242] 2 Tim 3:17.

13

Are There Individual Gifts Of Pastoring, Apostleship, And Evangelism?

In discussing the unity and maturing of believers, Paul describes in Ephesians 4 how God's comprehensive and unified work results in grace for each individual believer.[243] Each of us can rejoice, knowing that God has given us individually the grace we need, while at the same time we can understand that we are not independent of Him nor of each other. We are designed to function as His body – as one – even though we are individual members of His body.

Considering the unique source of grace and the gifts that stem from grace, Paul explains that Christ gave *the gift*,[244] and He gave *gifts*.[245] His grace included not just the singular gift of salvation,[246] but also everything necessary for complete sanctification.[247]

Ephesians 4:11 identifies four vital gifts: "and He gave *indeed* the apostles, and the prophets, and the

---

[243] Eph 4:7.
[244] Eph 4:7.
[245] Eph 4:8.
[246] As in Eph 2:8-9.
[247] As in Eph 2:10.

evangelists, and the pastors and teachers..." This is a literal translation accounting for each Greek word in the passage. Notice that the objects of the verb *gave* are preceded in each case by the definite article *the*. Also notice the passage does not say that He gave the gift of apostleship, prophecy, evangelism, and pastoring and teaching – if that is what Paul intended to say, he could have easily structured the passage to make that meaning clear. Instead, he identifies the gifts as the apostles themselves, the prophets themselves, the evangelists themselves, and the pastors and teachers themselves.

In other words, Ephesians 4:11 cannot be used exegetically to support the idea that, for example, there is a gift of evangelism. In fact, there isn't a single passage in Scripture that indicates evangelism requires a special gifting. All believers are given the mandate, as a part of the full armor of God, to have their feet shod "with the preparation of the gospel of peace."[248] Every believer is to be prepared and equipped with the gospel. Consequently, no one can claim their lack of the gift of evangelism as an excuse for their failure to faithfully share the gospel.

Further, Ephesians 4:11 does not advocate a gift of pastoring and teaching to individuals, either. The two terms share the same definite article, indicating that the two in this context are not to be understood as two separate functions, but as one. Pastors are not just pastors, they are pastors and teachers. Again, notice that it is not pastoring or teaching that is given *to the church* – the gift is the pastors and teachers themselves.

---

[248] Eph 6:15.

No other passage in Scripture supports pastoring as an individual gift, though teaching is identified as such in Romans 12:7.

In short, no one can claim accurately that they have been given special dispensation to be a pastor. Paul underscores this in 1 Timothy 3 when he explains that one can be appointed to the office of overseer if (1) he desires the office,[249] and (2) if he meets the qualifications as determined by those appointing him.[250] There is no spiritual gift in view in this passage, except for perhaps teaching. All the other characteristics are expected of every maturing believer.

Consequently, no aspiring pastor can excuse his own unpreparedness by appealing to a spiritual gift. And no functioning pastor can resist accountability based on his special choosing by God. The mentality that the pastor is "the Lord's anointed" likens pastors in the church to priests and even kings in Israel. Many a pastor has been shipwrecked because he failed to understand the difference between the administrative and leadership roles in theocratic and monarchial Israel and the pastoral role in the church – the two have nothing to do with each other.

Ephesians 4:11 is also not describing gifts of apostleship or prophecy. There is no passage in Scripture that describes apostleship as an individual and broadly applicable gift. Instead, Ephesians 4:11 notes that apostles themselves have been given to the church. These

---

[249] 1 Tim 3:1.
[250] 1 Tim 3:2-7.

apostles were handpicked by Him,[251] and had seen Jesus personally.[252] No one in the church today can claim these qualifications, nor can legitimately claim with any Biblical evidence that they have a gift of apostleship, for the Bible identifies no such gift. Paul calls those who make such a claim "false apostles, deceitful workers, disguising themselves as apostles of Christ."[253] Ouch. On the other hand, Ephesians 4:11 indicates that *the apostles* have been given to the church as a whole. Unlike apostleship, there is a spiritual gift of prophecy,[254] but that is not what is referred to in Ephesians 4:11. The reference there is to *the prophets* being given to the church.

Finally, it is vital that we realize why these gifts – the apostles, the prophets, the evangelists, and the pastors and teachers – were given to the church: "for the equipping of the saints for the work of service to the building up of the body of Christ."[255] God has given these gifts – or offices, if I may call them that – to the church in order for saints to be equipped, so that the body may be built up. It is also vital that we understand it is not these people that do the equipping, it is the word of God.[256]

These offices (or gifts to the church) have served the church (in the case of apostles and prophets) and continue to serve the church (in the case of evangelists and pastors and teachers) in ministries centered on God's

---

[251] Acts 1:2, 1 Cor 1:1.
[252] 1 Cor 9:1,15:7-9.
[253] 1 Cor 11:13.
[254] Rom 12:6.
[255] Eph 4:12.
[256] 2 Tim 3:16-17.

word. The goal is that each believer will one day be fully mature in Christ,[257] but until then we are called to no longer be children, carried about by every wind of doctrine. Biblical discernment requires that we base our understandings exclusively on what is written – even when what is written contradicts well established traditions and practices in the church. Considering Ephesians 4:11 gives us opportunity to do just that.

---

[257] Eph 4:13.

78   Gifted

14

The Peter Principles: Peter's Formula For Using Spiritual Gifts

There are four major Biblical contexts that discuss what we commonly refer to as spiritual gifts. In chronological order, they are 1 Corinthians 12-14, Romans 12:1-8, Paul's Letter to the Ephesians, and 1 Peter 4:10-11. It is notable that the explanations of spiritual gifts become increasingly simple as the New Testament progresses. 1 Corinthians 12-14 provides a very detailed discussion, especially of revelatory and sign gifts. Romans 12:1-8 builds on the grounding of the previous eleven chapters, and considers how gifts contribute to the overall functioning together of the body. Paul's Letter to the Ephesians focuses in the first three chapters on how the believer comes to have every spiritual blessing in the heavenlies in Christ, and what are the implications of those blessings. In the remaining three chapters, Paul challenges believers to walk in those blessings. Throughout the letter, Paul emphasizes the role of the Holy Spirit in the life of the believer. Finally, in 1 Peter 4:10-11, Peter offers a very simple formula for the use of gifts and their purpose.

By way of introduction, consider the intricacies of the combustion engine. How many of us have the knowledge to explain simply the interworking of the engine? Certainly a much smaller percentage of people understand those concepts than actually get behind the wheel and drive the car. Thankfully, our knowledge of how a car works does not have to extend to the details of engineering principles in order for us to have sufficient knowledge to drive.

Regarding spiritual gifts we discover a similar principle: there is actually not very much Biblical discussion of the nuts and bolts of spiritual gifts, yet believers are taught and exhorted to utilize these gifts properly. We aren't given the details of the combustion engine, yet we are given enough detail regarding how to operate the car that we can safely and efficiently operate the car and travel from one point to another. Of course, the more information we have the better, but not all information about the vehicle's anatomy is relevant to its end user operation. In short: the topic of spiritual gifts is far less complicated than we might think. Let's not complicate what God hasn't made complex.

Peter's commentary on gifts is brief and to the point. He begins, "as each has received a gift, employ it in serving one another as good stewards of the manifold grace of God."[258] The NASB translates the Greek charisma as a special gift. The KJV renders it the gift. Both translations take interpretive license. The NASB rendering assumes Peter is talking about individually

---

[258] 1 Pet 4:10.

distributed spiritual gifts, while the KJV assumes the gift is salvation. While the two translations attempt to qualify Peter's statement, there is no way to dogmatically identify from the (Greek) text which one of these ideas Peter intended. It is best that we simply recognize that each one has received a gift. That gift – whether salvation in general, or a more individual gift – is sufficient for the believer to be empowered to function as God designed. Peter doesn't give details of the combustion engine, but he does expect believers to drive the car properly. Believers are to use the gift in serving one another, and this serving is good stewardship of God's diverse and manifold grace.

Incidentally, that last phrase of 4:10 includes the Greek *poikiles*, meaning diverse or manifold. The inclusion of the term seems to imply that Peter is considering individually distributed and various aspects of grace, rather than the grace of salvation. But again, we cannot be dogmatic on this point. Either way, we are told how to employ the gift: serving one another, and thereby being good stewards of what He has given.

In the next verse, Peter describes two kinds of activities based on the gift: speaking and serving. "Whoever speaks, as one who is speaking the words of God; whoever serves, as one who is serving by the strength which God supplies."[259] This exhortation does not specify what to do when speaking and serving, but rather how to do it. Our words should be consistent with the words of God, and our serving should be with diligence as empowered by Him. Simple. Peter presents

---

[259] 1 Pet 4:11a.

the purpose of the gift and the employment of the gift in 4:11b: "so that in all things God may be glorified through Jesus Christ, to whom belongs the glory and dominion forever and ever. Amen." Again, this is very simple. The purpose is theocentric and doxological – centered on Him and for His glory.

Peter's principles, then, for gifts are as follows:

(1) Each has a gift to be used for serving others.
(2) Proper use of the gift(s) is necessary for good stewardship of the grace we have been given.
(3) Speaking is proper if it is consistent with the words of God.
(4) Serving is to be with diligence as empowered by God.
(5) The purpose for all this is His glory.

15

What is Speaking in Tongues? Part 1

Besides a mention in the disputed ending of Mark,[260] we are first introduced to *tongues*[261] in the book of Acts, where we find three historical occurrences of people who spoke in tongues. In Acts 2:3-4, when the church was born at Pentecost, tongues served in part as evidence that the Holy Spirit was present as Jesus promised He would be.[262] Jewish believers were "filled with the Holy Spirit and began to speak with other tongues..."[263]

They were literally proclaiming the Gospel in various languages that they had not learned.[264] Later, in Acts 10:44-46, gentile believers also received the Holy Spirit in the same way, and before they were even water baptized[265] they spoke in tongues and exalted God. Finally, in Acts 19:1-7, there were about twelve believers

---

[260] Mk 16:17, in which Jesus describes tongues as a sign accompanying belief.
[261] Greek, *glossa*.
[262] Acts 1:5.
[263] Greek, *heterais glossais*.
[264] Acts 2:9-11.
[265] Acts 10:47.

who weren't present at Pentecost, and who were unaware that the Holy Spirit had been given.[266] After being baptized, and after Paul laid hands upon them, they began to speak in tongues and prophecy.[267]

These are the only three recorded historical instances of tongues in the New Testament. The only other discussion regarding tongues as a gift or as related to the ministry of the Holy Spirit, besides Mark 16:17, is found in 1 Corinthians 12-14. Whereas in Acts we see a few historical instances of tongues, in 1 Corinthians we find the only explanatory content about tongues. 1 Corinthians 12:10 characterizes tongues and the interpretation of tongues as manifestations of the Spirit for the common good.[268] In 12:28-30 Paul discusses tongues in the context of diversity of ministries: not all speak in tongues or interpret them.

To this point in the history of the early church, up to 1 Corinthians 12, tongues was *only defined in Acts 2*, and was clearly proclaiming the gospel in languages the speaker had not learned. With no further expansion of that definition, Paul has described tongues in 1 Corinthians 12 as a contemporary manifestation of the Spirit. So it is notable that Paul introduces 13:1 by saying "If I speak with the tongues of men and of angels..." Does this phrase constitute an expansion of the definition of tongues? Is there an application of tongues that involves speaking with the tongues of angels?

---

[266] Acts 19:2.
[267] Acts 19:6.
[268] 1 Cor 12:7.

Paul may be using a literary device called *hyperbole,* from two Greek words together meaning *to overthrow.* It is an exaggeration to make a point. To understand whether or not this introductory clause is hyperbole, let's consider the structure of 13:1-3. Introducing 13:2 and 13:3 are similar conditional clauses employing the Greek *ean,* or if. In 13:2 Paul says, "If I...know all mysteries and knowledge..." In 13:9 Paul says "we know in part," using the same root for *knowledge* as in 13:2. This is a straightforward admission that Paul recognizes he does not have all knowledge.

The conditional phrase of 13:2 is *hyperbole.* Paul is not writing of something that is reality. In 13:3 we read, "If I surrender my body to be burned..." Paul had not done this, and would not do it in the future. Church history is agreed that Paul was martyred by beheading. Again, Paul seems to be using hyperbole. In 13:1 the phrase *tongues of angels* is likely hyperbole as well. We cannot say this dogmatically, but there is no textual or historical evidence that the gift of tongues somehow involved angelic languages.

In fact, in every Biblical instance of angels speaking to or in front of human listeners those listeners always *understood* what was said. Also, in this context Paul's purpose is not to expound on the gift of tongues, but rather to show the superiority of love over and against tongues and other actions and gifts. It would be odd, though not impossible, for Paul to introduce new data about the characteristics of tongues when the context is *deemphasizing* rather than extolling tongues.

To illustrate the superiority of love over tongues, Paul draws the contrast in 13:8, saying, "Love never fails...if there are tongues, they will cease..." It is evident that tongues were temporary, but more on that later. To review, so far in 1 Corinthians Paul has characterized tongues as a contemporary (to his time) manifestation of the Holy Spirit for the common good,[269] and has argued that tongues are inferior to love and are temporary.[270]

In 14:2 Paul makes the strange statement that "one who speaks in a tongue does not speak to men but to God; for no one understands, but in spirit he speaks mysteries." In this context Paul is extolling prophecy *over the way the Corinthians were using tongues*.[271] In 14:4 Paul adds, "one who speaks in a tongue edifies himself; but one who prophesies edifies the church." It appears, based on Paul's hypothetical statement in 14:4, that the Corinthians were *not using tongues as they were intended*, but were somehow using them for self-edification.[272]

At this point we should take note that we have not yet been told the purpose of tongues; so far we only know from this discourse that spiritual gifts are for broad benefit rather than self-edification. It is in this context that Paul ranks tongues and prophecy. In 14:5 he says, "I wish that you all spoke in tongues, but even more that you would prophesy; and greater is one who prophesies than one who speaks in tongues, unless he interprets, so

---

[269] 1 Cor 12.
[270] 1 Cor 13.
[271] 1 Cor 14:9-12.
[272] Perhaps doing so in the name of prayer (14:14).

that the church may receive edifying." Paul explains that prophecy is a superior gift to the Corinthians' use of tongues because prophecy would edify the entire body, whereas tongues was apparently being used at Corinth with no concern for church edification.

In 14:6 Paul uses himself as an example: "But now, brethren, if I come to you speaking in tongues, what will I profit you unless I speak to you either by way of revelation or of knowledge or of prophecy or of teaching?" He notes the importance of uttering "by the tongue speech that is clear," otherwise what is spoken cannot be known.[273] He further confirms in 14:9-11 the idea that a tongue was a language to be understood, but acknowledges that not all would know the languages being used: "Therefore let one who speaks in a tongue pray that he may interpret."[274]

In Acts 2:7 those who understood the dialects being spoken were amazed and astonished, but in 2:13, those who did not understand what was said were mocking and assuming the tongues-speakers were drunk. Those who understood were edified, but those who didn't weren't. Paul's desire for the Corinthians was that they all be edified. Consequently if a tongue was used it should be interpreted so that there would not be confusion.

To this point in 1 Corinthians 14 there has been nothing to suggest that tongues involved anything but various human languages or dialects; nor is there any support for tongues as a self-edifying gift. But in 14:14 Paul hypothesizes: "For if I pray in a tongue, my spirit

---

[273] 1 Cor 14:9.
[274] 1 Cor 14:13.

prays but my mind is unfruitful." Once again we must consider whether Paul is speaking of a real and proper use of tongues or if he has returned to his earlier use of hyperbole.

So far in this context (chs. 13-14) Paul has used the Greek *ean* (if) to introduce hypothetical or hyperbolic clauses. "If I pray in a tongue"[275] has the same basic structure and function as "If I speak with the tongues of men and of angels" in 13:1.[276] If the conditional clauses of 13:1-3 are to be understood as hyperbole, then so should the conditional clause of 14:14. In the hypothetical scenario of praying in tongues in 14:14 only the spirit is praying. But in 14:15 Paul advocates for praying both with the mind and the spirit. In short, *he is renouncing prayer in tongues*, because while it would hypothetically be a good way to give thanks, it does not edify the other person.[277]

If tongues was intended to be used for prayer, God would be able to understand what was being said. So *in theory* it could work in that capacity, but Paul gives no indication here or anywhere else that tongues is intended for prayer. Nonetheless, it is from these passages that some conclude the gift of tongues is intended for prayer. Normally those who draw that conclusion will not regard any of the conditional clauses of chapters 13-14 as hyperbole, but will view them as legitimate possibilities (and realities). Consequently, it is taught by some that the gift of tongues involves potentially both prayer and

---

[275] Greek, *ean gar proseuxomai glosse.*
[276] Greek, *ean tais glossais ton anthropon lalo kai ton allelon.*
[277] 1 Cor 14:17.

angelic languages. It is evident that recognizing the meaning of the conditional clauses in this context is central for understanding the use of tongues. That Paul intends them in a hyperbolic sense is consistent with the syntax, discursive structure, and theological argument of the immediate context.

As Paul continues the discussion in 14:18 he avoids the implication that he is renouncing tongues entirely, as he acknowledges his own superlative use of tongues. He reiterates the importance of utilizing both mind and spirit and of instructing in an understandable way.[278] Paul doesn't want the Corinthians to stop using tongues; he wants them to use the gift properly and for the right reasons. In the context of the church he would rather speak fewer words with his mind rather than many in tongues so that others might understand and be edified.

After exhorting the Corinthians to be mature in their thinking,[279] Paul explains the purpose for the gift of tongues, quoting Isaiah 28:11-12, and loosely referencing the Law of God – His word – rather than the Law of Moses – the Torah section of the Hebrew Bible: "By men of strange tongues and by the lips of strangers I will speak to this people and even so they will not listen to Me." Paul reminds the Corinthians in 14:22 of God's preannounced plans and then explains tongues specifically: *"So then tongues are for a sign, not to those who believe, but to unbelievers."*

Isaiah 28:11-12 explains in the context of Israel's judgment that God had in the past used foreigners or

---

[278] 1 Cor 14:19.
[279] 1 Cor 14:20.

gentiles to accomplish his purpose – even to illustrate God's character and grace. For example, God extended grace to pagan Nineveh during Jonah's ministry, and the people of Nineveh repented.[280] In the same way as He did then (and in other instances) God would use gentiles to illustrate His character and grace: tongues would be a sign for unbelieving Jews, specifically, that God had indeed poured out His grace. It is notable that most of the dialects and languages[281] represented in Acts 2:8-11 were gentile dialects. In a sense, gentile believers would even provide impetus for Israel to believe in her Messiah.[282] Tongues, then, served a prophetic purpose and also a practical one.

In the practical sense tongues helped confirm God's message and that His hand was in this new work, the church. Throughout Biblical history God has used signs, miracles, and wonders to confirm His message and His work – first with Moses, then with Elijah and Elisha, then with certain prophets, including the two still yet to come, then with Christ himself, and finally with the apostles and prophets in the early church. Also still yet in the future we anticipate Satan's counterfeit of signs, miracles, and wonders, as he will seek to deceive many.[283] Each of these periods of signs, miracles, and wonders were specifically purposed and very, very brief.

While tongues did serve a practical purpose, Paul's concern in 1 Corinthians 14 is the prophetic purpose: to

---

[280] Jon 3:5-10.
[281] Greek, *dialekto*.
[282] Rom 11:11-14.
[283] Rev 13:11-15.

illustrate for Israel what Peter had so boldly proclaimed in Acts 2:22-36 – that God had sent His Messiah, and that Messiah was the Lord Jesus Christ. Consequently, and with that prophetic purpose in mind, if the Corinthians were using tongues in any way not conducive with edification of the church in a broad sense, its purpose would go unfulfilled. If an ungifted person[284] or an unbeliever[285] entered the assembly and tongues were used with no interpreter, then the response would be ultimately the same as in Acts 2:13 – that those who were speaking were drunk or insane.[286]

In 1 Corinthians 12 Paul explains that tongues is a legitimate manifestation of the Holy Spirit. In chapter 13 he explains that love is superior to tongues and other gifts, and that tongues is temporary. In the early sections of chapter 14 he explains the problems with misuse of tongues. Concluding chapter 14 he explains in simple terms how tongues should be used. All spiritual gifts are to be used for the edification[287] – and consistent with his earlier message, that means edification of the church, not self-edification.[288]

Tongues should be spoken by two or three at the most, each in turn, and one must interpret.[289] If there is no one to interpret then tongues may not be used,[290] but instead the person should speak to himself and to God.

---

[284] Greek, *idiotai*.
[285] Greek, *apistoi*.
[286] 1 Cor 14:23.
[287] 1 Cor 14:26.
[288] 1 Cor 14:1-19.
[289] 1 Cor 14:27.
[290] 1 Cor 14:28.

This last clause is especially notable because of its implications for tongues as a means of prayer. While the person, in the church, is to speak to himself and God,[291] he is to be silent in the church.[292] In other words, if there is no interpreter, the person should speak *silently* to himself and God. This is further evidence that tongues was not to be used for prayer, but that *prayer was to be engaged instead of speaking in tongues.*

Finally, in 14:39 Paul exhorts the Corinthians not to prevent or forbid speaking in tongues,[293] and in 14:40 he concludes by reiterating that all things must be done properly and in good order. It is notable that Paul directly addresses the Corinthians as *adelphoi*, or brothers in 14:39 and uses the present active imperative in his exhortation. He does not give these instructions to the Ephesians or the Galatians or any other local church. His instructions are specific to the Corinthian church. Now, of course, that does not mean other churches could not draw a secondary application that tongues had a valid role in the church, but we must be careful not to extrapolate that command as specifically and necessarily involving all believers without further textual warrant. Note how specifically Paul uses the term *adelphoi* in 1 Corinthians, especially in 1:11, 2:1, 3:1, 4:6, etc.

Combining all that data we have on tongues, including Mark 16:1, Acts 2, 10, and 19, and 1 Corinthians 12-14, we may conclude that tongues was a miraculous gift given for confirmation specifically to

---

[291] Greek, *heauto de laleito kai to theo.*
[292] Greek, *oigato en ekklesia.*
[293] Greek, *to lalein me koluete glossais.*

Israel that God had poured out His Spirit in the same manner as in Joel 2, though not in fulfillment of that passage, as a further confirmation that the Messiah had indeed come. In examining these passages we discover that tongues was very limited in its usage, with only three recorded occurrences, and that the conditions were not always the same. For example, in Acts 2 there was no water baptism in context, in Acts 10, speaking in tongues occurred before water baptism, and in Acts 19 it occurred after. We further learn that there was temptation to use the gift improperly, as the Corinthians were apparently doing. To correct that error Paul explains the scope, purpose, and proper application of the gift. Any usage outside the parameters discussed by Paul in this brief context of 1 Corinthians 12-14 simply cannot be legitimately considered a *Biblical application* of the gift.

Finally, it is notable that after Paul's teaching in 1 Corinthians, written around 54-55 AD, there is no further mention in the entire New Testament of the gift of tongues. Not even in Paul's soon-to-follow second letter to the Corinthians, did he mention the gift. The notable absence of any further mentions during the remaining forty years of Biblical history, coupled with timestamp passages like 1 Corinthians 13:8-10, Ephesians 2:20, 4:11-13, and Hebrews 2:2-4, begs us to consider whether the gift of tongues is foundational, fulfilled, and no longer active in the church, or whether the gift is enduring and believers have access to it in the contemporary church.

16

What is Speaking in Tongues? Part 2

There are four key Biblical concepts that give us insight into the perpetuation of the gift of tongues — specifically, that the gift has fulfilled its purpose and is no longer a factor for the church today. First is the nature, purpose, and scope of signs miracles and wonders in the Bible. Second is the Ephesians 2:19-20 and 4:11-13 illustration of the church as a building composed of particular parts. Third is a remarkable admission by the author of Hebrews in 2:2-4 of the foundational nature of signs, miracles, and wonders. And finally, there is specific discussion regarding how and when tongues would cease in 1 Corinthians 13:8-12. The first three are considered in this chapter. 1 Corinthians 13:8-12 is handled in detail in a later chapter.

Signs, Miracles, and Wonders

God used signs, miracles, and wonders throughout Biblical history for specific purposes and in very limited contexts. The first period was during the ministry of Moses,[294] but no miracles by human hands[295] are recorded

---

[294] E.g., Ex 3:20, 7:3.

in Joshua – the chronological book immediately following the lifetime of Moses. And just a few years after Joshua's time, Gideon speaks of miracles as if they are long since past,[296] even though God is willing to show him a sign.[297]

The second period was during the ministries of Elijah and Elisha, though their ministries were never specifically referred to using the terms signs, miracles, or wonders. Still we see during their ministries miraculous deeds that they did which confirmed their messages.[298] The third period was the ministry of Jesus, and all three terms are used to describe the evidence for His identity and message.[299] Fourth, was the apostolic era,[300] in which the apostles' message was confirmed by divine evidence.[301]

Further, various prophets were used of God to do miraculous things, especially the still yet future two prophets of Revelation 11:3-6. Notably, their miraculous ministries are very brief. Finally, the last Biblical period of miracles is during the time of the one we call antichrist. He will be filled "with all power and signs and false wonders."[302] In each case where there are authentic signs, miracles, or wonders, they occur with preannounced or confirmed authority.[303] *In each case also*

---

[295] The miracles in Joshua (Jos 3:10-17, 4:18, 6:6-20, 10:12-14) were not by human agency.
[296] Judg 6:13.
[297] Judg 6:17.
[298] 1 Kin 17:18-23, 2 Kin 5:15.
[299] Acts 2:22.
[300] E.g., 2 Cor 12:12.
[301] E.g., Heb 2:4.
[302] 2 Thes 2:8-9.
[303] Ex 3:20, 1 Kin 17, Acts 2:22, Rev 11:3-6, 2 Cor 12:12.

the signs, miracles, and wonders never advanced beyond the generation in which they began. In other words, the precedent and resulting expectation regarding signs, miracles, and wonders was that they were very purposed and very temporary. That there might be some miraculous activity or commissioning that would last for centuries was not the expectation of any context of Scripture.

The Church as a House (Eph 2:19-20; 4:11-12)

Paul describes the church metaphorically as "God's house" in Ephesians 2:19. Filling out the word picture, Paul identifies two additional key components of the house: Christ Jesus as the cornerstone, and the foundation as the apostles and prophets. In Jesus, the whole building is growing into a holy temple, and believers are being built together into a dwelling of God in the Spirit.[304] In this building there are three directly cited phases of construction: the corner, the foundation, and the building up of the building. Notice that the foundation does not precede the corner, and the building up does not precede the foundation. Further, it is noteworthy that apostles and prophets are the foundation – the singular antecedent, *foundation*,[305] identifies that both the apostolic and prophetic offices are foundational.

Basic architectural principles require that the foundation be completed before the whole building is built up. That the apostles and prophets were described as foundational implies that there would be an end to their

---

[304] Eph 2:21-22.
[305] Greek, *themelio*.

ministry, and that the building would necessarily progress *past them*. That progress is considered in Ephesians 4:11-12 when once again apostles and prophets are mentioned, but this time those offices are followed in context by evangelists and pastors and teachers.

Paul returns in 4:12 to the architectural metaphor, identifying in 4:11 evangelists and pastors and teachers as non-foundational – in other words, as the offices necessary not for the foundation, but for the building up of the body. It is notable that Paul uses a mixed metaphor. First using architectural language – building up in 4:12, then body terminology – the body of Christ, also in 4:12, then reference to human maturity or completeness in 4:13-14. This illustrates Paul's penchant for using multiple and mixed metaphors to illustrate a major point. He uses the same literary device in the pivotal 1 Corinthians 13:8-12. But before we consider the Corinthian context, we take note of another New Testament writer who understood signs, miracles, and wonders as foundational and very temporary.

The Hebrews Admission

The writer of Hebrews describes salvation as "first being spoken through the Lord," and then as "confirmed to us by those who heard." The author makes it clear that he was not a firsthand witness of the Lord's message. The confirmation came to "us" by those who heard. The writer acknowledges being a second-generation believer in a sense, and not an apostle. He further recognizes that God worked uniquely through the apostles – "those who heard." God testified with them "both by signs and wonders and by various miracles and by gifts of the Holy Spirit according to His own will." Adding to the more common signs, miracles, and wonders terminology, the author includes the phrase "gifts of the Holy Spirit." The Greek *merismois* (not *charisma*, in this case) is perhaps better translated as *distributions*. This does not refer to the Holy Spirit as the gift or distribution, in contrast to passages like Acts 2:38 in which the Spirit is referred to as *ten dorean* – the gift). God used gifts or distributions of the Holy Spirit in the Apostles to confirm His message.

17

Does Speaking in Tongues Prove That We Have the Holy Spirit?

With over 40,000 members, Lakewood Church in Houston, Texas is the largest church in the United States. For better or for worse, Lakewood and its leader Joel Osteen are profoundly influential. One significant area of influence is in the realm of spiritual gifts. A search of the terms "spiritual gifts" on Lakewood's website produced (at the top of the list) a downloadable booklet called *Understanding the Baptism of the Holy Spirit*, from Joel Osteen Ministries, and authored by Lisa Comes.

The booklet explains how and why one should speak in tongues, and cites speaking in tongues as evidence of the baptism of the Holy Spirit.[306] The view promoted in the booklet is not original with Lakewood, Osteen, or Comes – in fact, it is the prevailing view in Pentecostal and Charismatic denominations. But is it a Biblical view? Is speaking in tongues needed evidence that we have the Holy Spirit?

First, as we considered earlier, Romans 8:9 emphatically notes that, "if anyone does not have the

---

[306] Lisa Comes, *Understanding the Baptism of the Holy Spirit* (Houston, TX: Joel Osteen Ministries), Point 5, page 3.

Spirit of Christ, he does not belong to Him." By contrast Osteen's and Comes' booklet cites Acts 2:17-19, 39, Luke 11:13, and John 7:37-39 to support the point that not every believer has the Holy Spirit. And it is true that Romans presents a very different picture of how one receives the Holy Spirit than do the Gospels and even the book of Acts. But rather than contradicting one another, these books consider different contexts, different times, and different ways in which God has worked over the ages. There is nothing contradictory there at all.

To illustrate, Joel Osteen has never, to my knowledge, advocated that believers today should present to the Lord two turtledoves or two young pigeons as is mandated in Leviticus 5:7. Presumably this is because Osteen recognizes that Leviticus was written about a different people and context than the church of today. If we recognize there are distinctions between audiences, times, and contexts in the Bible, then we should be very diligent to recognize those distinctions in our Bible study. We should not be careless or hasty in proclaiming what the Bible does and does not say. We should not apply what God said specifically for someone else's benefit to ourselves, unless there is direct exegetical warrant to do so, otherwise, we are saying "Thus says the Lord" when thus *hasn't* said the Lord. And that's obviously a sizable problem. In dealing with the issue of the Holy Spirit and spiritual gifts we need to first understand, and not ignore, the distinctions in the Bible.

Second, if the Bible is not teaching that speaking in tongues is necessary evidence that we have the Holy Spirit, then we need to take a look at *what the Bible says is evidence* of the Holy Spirit in us. Romans 8:9 describes how every believer in Christ from that time forward has the Holy Spirit. Ephesians 1:13-14 describes how believers are sealed in Him with the Holy Spirit who was promised, and how He is given as a down payment (or pledge) of our inheritance. 1 Corinthians 12:13 explains that believers are all baptized by the Spirit into the body of Christ. Every believer in Christ, at least from the time 1 Corinthians was written, has been baptized by the Holy Spirit. In light of these passages, the real question is not what evidences that the Holy Spirit is in us. Paul's statements address that issue decisively. No, the real question is what evidences that we are believers in Jesus Christ. Because if we are in Christ, we have His Spirit. We know that if we are in Him, He is in us. But how can we be sure we are in Him?

This question is a major reason John wrote his first epistle. 1 John 5:13 gives one of his purpose statements for writing the letter: "These things I have written to you who believe in the name of the Son of God, so that you may know that you have eternal life." So that you may *know*. It is fascinating that in a letter written to believers to give them assurance – evidence – of their salvation, that never once does John mention baptism or spiritual gifts of any kind. He does, on the other hand, offer three evidences:

Evidence #1: Our Love

"By this we know that we have come to know Him, if we keep His commandments [love God, love your neighbor]...whoever keeps His word...By this we know that we are in Him"³⁰⁷ ... "We know that we have passed out of death into life because we love the brethren."³⁰⁸

Evidence #2: When Our Love Fails, He Does Not
"We will know by this [love] that we are of the truth, *and will assure our heart before Him in whatever our heart condemns us; for God is greater than our heart and knows all things.*"³⁰⁹

Evidence #3: The Spirit Whom He Has Given Us
"We know by this that He abides in us, *by the Spirit whom He has given us*"³¹⁰..."By this we know that we abide in Him and He in us, because He has given us of His Spirit."³¹¹ In these three ways, every believer can be confident of his or her position in Christ. The expression of love, and not some mystical gift, is our visible evidence of whose we are. When our love is insufficient and fails, He reminds us that we are His anyway.³¹² His Spirit within us is another proof of our position in Him – not evidenced by any mystical manifestation, but simply by His presence, affirmed by the word of God.

Consequently, if we insist that manifestations of spiritual gifts are needed evidence of our salvation, then we commit at least two errors: (1) we misunderstand the function and purpose of spiritual gifts (for edification, not for evidence of position), and (2) we deprive believers of

---

[307] 1 Jn 2:3-5.
[308] 1 Jn 3:14.
[309] 1 Jn 3:19-20.
[310] 1 Jn 3:24.
[311] 1 Jn 4:13.
[312] E.g., Rom 8:1, 28-39.

the Biblical means of assurance and certainty. Once we have believed, our position in Christ is no longer a matter of faith – it is a matter of which we can be certain, according to John. There is great encouragement in that.

106   Gifted

18

On Possibility and Certainty In Biblical Interpretation

As I was writing this chapter, in another room my Lovely Bride quizzed our Youngest Daughter on her spelling words (including the word "duck"). Meanwhile, Oldest Daughter studied at her desk and was just about to get up from her desk and walk to the room where the following dialogue would take place. Lovely Bride paused to ask me a question. The dialogue want something like this:

Lovely Bride (to me): Spell "duck"

Me (looking up from my work, and answering loudly and with authority, because I was confident I knew the answer): d–u–c–k... DUCK.

Lovely Bride (chuckling): Would you like some oatmeal?

Me: That would be great, thank you!

> Oldest Daughter (just entering the room): Daddy, why don't you like oatmeal?
> Me (puzzled): I never said that...
>
> Oldest Daughter (puzzled): But do you like the way it tastes?
>
> Me (still puzzled): Well, yeah...why?
> Oldest Daughter (still puzzled): But I just heard you say oatmeal was "YUCK."

This brief conversation (even as I was writing an article on the importance of context) served as a timely reminder to me of the importance of context in any discussion. In this simple exchange my lovely daughter concluded the exact opposite of the truth because she was only privy to part of the context. Thankfully, she dug a little deeper to arrive at the correct answer. Of course, oatmeal and ducks are unimportant compared to God's communication in Scripture, and unfortunately, we sometimes draw conclusions without digging deep enough in the context.

An excellent question was recently posed to me on this topic, and it went like this:

> In handling 1 Corinthians 13 you have suggested that the conditional clauses including *ean* were hyperbolic, but in several instances the clause appears *not* to be hyperbolic: 1 Corinthians 9:16 ("if I preach the gospel" – which Paul did), 10:28 (meat sacrificed to idols was very plausible), 14:6

("if I come to you speaking in tongues"), and 15:36 ("that which you sow does not come to life unless it dies" – plausible). How can you conclude that 13:1 (tongues of angels) is hyperbolic?

In doing exegesis, we understand that many conclusions are *possible*, but we have a responsibility to understand the distinction between *possible* and *certain*. Here's what I mean: I can read Genesis 1:1 and assert the possibility that God also created life on other planets. I have to admit that the narrow context of Genesis 1:1 does not eliminate that possibility. But is Genesis 1:1 asserting that God created life on other planets? Of course not. While there is a possibility, there is no certainty, and so I cannot use that passage to teach that there is life on other planets. *We must explore other contexts.*

Here is another example: in classical dispensational theology, some tried to account for an old earth by inserting an indefinite timeframe (perhaps millions of years) between Genesis 1:1 and 1:2. Does the text itself allow for such a timeframe? It certainly doesn't immediately and directly eliminate that possibility, but it also does not at all support that possibility as a certainty. So in order to have certainty on the issue of whether there is a time gap between Genesis 1:1 and 1:2 *we must explore other contexts.*

Consequently, even though there is a textual possibility in one immediate context, the introduction of other (related, of course) contexts helps us to move from possibility to certainty – either in favor of or in opposition to a particular conclusion. In other words, before we draw a conclusion regarding certainty in any passage, *we must earn it exegetically*. This is a vital principle in Biblical interpretation.

Regarding the question of life on other planets, passages like Psalm 19:1–4 help us to understand God's purpose in creating things we can't physically access, but doesn't give us certainty one way or another about otherworldly life. I would suggest the Bible doesn't directly answer that question (consequently, it would not surprise me or upset the Biblical worldview to discover life elsewhere, and even if I may not expect to find life elsewhere, the investigation is worthwhile). Regarding the question of the time gap in Genesis 1, there is a direct answer. In Exodus 20:11 and 31:17 all the events of Genesis 1 are described as taking place in six days. If we understand those six days in the plain sense, then we have certainty on the issue – that there is no time gap in Genesis 1.

The same principle is in play with the conditional clauses of 1 Corinthians 13 (as it is in every other passage of Scripture). 1 Corinthians 9:16 includes the conditional clause, "if I proclaim the Gospel." From this verse we understand it is a *possibility* that Paul preached the Gospel, but we are not informed in this context whether it is a *certainty*. In order to have certainty one way or another, we must examine other contexts. From passages like Romans 15:9, 1 Corinthians 15:1–2, 2 Corinthians 11:7, and Galatians 1:11, we conclude with certainty that, yes, Paul preached the Gospel.

In 1 Corinthians 10:28 includes the clause, "But if anyone says to you." Can we know from 10:28 whether or

Possibility and Certainty in Biblical Interpretation 111

not anyone said ("This is meat sacrificed to idols") to them? No. There is nothing in the verse itself that gives us that information. So we examine other contexts in order to discover if we can have certainty or not. While in 1 Corinthians there are several references to things sacrificed to idols,[313] there is no definitive statement that such a statement had actually been made to the Corinthians.

Of course it is very plausible that such a statement had been made, but we can only recognize it as plausible because of the prominence of the concept (of things sacrificed to idols) in Paul's letter to the Corinthians. Hence, we may move from *possibility* to *plausibility*, but we must stop short of *certainty* in this instance – for to assert certainty *we would have to go beyond what is written, and we cannot do that and at the same time claim to be exegetical in our method.*

In 1 Corinthians 14:6 Paul says, "If I come to you speaking in tongues." From 14:6 we cannot conclude whether he did or did not speak in tongues at Corinth. In 14:18 he acknowledges that he did speak in tongues, but in 14:19 he adds that in the church, the assembly, he would rather not. From this context it is not certain that Paul ever came to the Corinthian church speaking in tongues, but it would seem unlikely in light of his communicated preference.[314] So the condition of 14:6 is *possible*, and even *plausible*, but is *unlikely*.

In 1 Corinthians 15:36 Paul uses the clause, ("That which you sow does not come to life...") "...unless it dies."

---

[313] E.g., 8:1, 4, 7, 10, 10:19, and 28.
[314] 1 Cor 14:19.

Does Paul write with the expectation that what is sown will die? We cannot know from 15:36, but in an earlier context, Paul argues that Christ was raised from the dead,[315] and that all who are in Christ will also be made alive in the same way.[316] Consequently, it is evident that in order for resurrection to occur, there must be death.[317] Yet in asserting the general certainty of death preceding resurrection, Paul introduces an exceptional case of resurrection preceded by a putting off of the mortal, yet without death[318] – I identify this as a clear reference to the event we call the *rapture*. In any case, the conditional clause of 15:36 can be understood from near contexts as referring not only to something that is both possible and plausible, but is, in fact certain, with only one exceptional scenario (i.e., rapture).

In these conditional clauses we have examples of at least *possible, plausible, unlikely, likely,* and *certain* (both negative and positive). When we arrive at the conditional clause introducing 13:1, the same considerations are in view. The clause reads: "If I speak with the tongues of men and of angels..." Take special note that in the Greek the verb comes after "of the men" and before "and of the angels." The clause could be translated: "If with the tongues of the men I speak and of the angels..." Word order matters here, and the separation of the two objects (the men, and the angels) by the verb could be significant.

---

[315] 1 Cor 15:20.
[316] 1 Cor 15:22.
[317] 1 Cor 15:42-46.
[318] 1 Cor 15:51-56.

Possibility and Certainty in Biblical Interpretation   113

There are two possibilities: (1) since Paul uses the verb only once in the clause, the implication could be that the tongues of men and angels were the same, (2) since Paul separates the two with the verb, they ought to be understood as distinct. From 13:1 we cannot be certain that either possibility is the correct understanding. Again, we have to rely on other contexts. Notably, 1 Corinthians 13:1 is the only reference in Scripture to tongues of angels. So we can make no certain statements regarding whether tongues of men and angels are distinct from each other or identical.

If the two are identical, then a practical question may be resolved: tongues of men, to that point, were identifiable human languages,[319] and every tongue (or sound) had its distinct meaning.[320] If tongues of men and angels are identical, then there can be no case made that tongues of angels had no discernible meaning. Angels would have simply spoken in human languages, or men would have spoken in angelic languages. However, if the two are different (as I take them to be), then the use of the two objects separated by the verb could indicate that the phrase "and of the angels" is a hyperbolic tack-on.

We already know that Paul spoke in tongues, even though he didn't announce that fact until 14:18, but there is no other Biblical context upon which we may rely that indicates any data whatsoever about tongues of angels. Absent of such data, we cannot conclude it certain, likely, or even plausible that such a condition – people speaking with tongues of angels – existed. Instead, we can only see

---

[319] E.g., Acts 2:8-11.
[320] 1 Cor 14:10-11.

it as possible, and then only if the conditional clause itself doesn't preclude the possibility.

It is also notable that Paul adds, "...but do not have love" to the condition. The hypothetical issue is not merely the speaking in certain kinds of tongues, but the speaking in those kinds of tongues *without love*. It is an if/then proposition. If there is speaking without love, then there is only a noisy gong or clanging cymbal. So the question is not whether Paul spoke in tongues, but whether Paul spoke in tongues *without love*. Was that possible? Certainly. Was it plausible? We have no exegetical data to support whether or not Paul ever did such a thing,

Consequently, Paul is not presenting the clause (the speaking without love) as something *he had done*, but rather as a hypothetical for the Corinthians to consider. The additional phrase "and of angels" would elevate the hypothetical to a superlative degree – much like Paul's conditional reference in Galatians 1:8 to an angel from heaven preaching a contrary gospel, Is it possible that an angel from heaven did or would do such a thing? From Galatians 1:8 we cannot rule it out, but to assert it as plausible, likely, or certain would require exegetical evidence (of an angel preaching falsely to the Galatians) – evidence we don't have. Paul's purpose is not to warn the Galatians against angels who would come to them bearing false gospels, but to warn them of the authority of the true gospel, that falsehoods are not worthy to offset the truth of the gospel the Galatians had received.

In like manner, the introduction to 1 Corinthians 13 is hypothetical, with the phrase "and of angels" extending the hypothetical to the superlative degree. The primary application for the Corinthians was that no matter how superlative their gifting, it was worthless without love. The grammatical structure supports this. The data in the context and the absence of data in other contexts supports this, and other instances of Pauline hypothetical and hyperbole supports this.

To assert to the contrary that Paul is suggesting believers can speak with the tongues of angels, and to extrapolate that assertion into a doctrine of tongues which includes tongues of angels as prayer languages and for other purposes, is to engage in an eisegetical fallacy. One might make an argument from a singular isolated context; in the light of such limited context a theory might be *possible*, but to ignore related contexts and still maintain the idea as *plausible*, *likely*, or *certain*, we go far beyond what is written in trying to defend a theological point. And, after all, what is more important – our theological viewpoints or God's communication in Scripture? Hopefully we will conform those viewpoints to what is actually written in God's word.

19

Purpose, and the Corinthians' Use of Tongues

In employing the literal grammatical-historical hermeneutic we acknowledge *the progress of revelation.* Though Acts 2 was written probably more than ten years after Paul's first letter to the Corinthians, the events described in Acts 2 took place, however, as many as eighteen years before Paul's letter was penned. The Corinthians would have likely been quite familiar with the event.

Note that Paul discusses the concept with them as if they understood what he was talking about. It is worth noting that Paul uses the term *glossa,* or *tongues,* sixteen times in 1 Corinthians before any definition or purpose is offered in chapter 14:22. It would be strange for Paul to speak of an issue repeatedly without expecting that his readers would already have at least some preliminary understanding. Of course this is not conclusive one way or the other, but when we observe the cumulative case here it seems quite consistent with the understanding of progressive revelation (that Paul is relying on earlier definition).

Further, in chapter 14, the content is not *what*, but *how*. There is no purpose for tongues cited until 14:22, but only a discussion of how tongues is to be used. Further, in 14:14 praying in a tongue (even if not hyperbolic, as I understand it to be) is not encouraged, but rather Paul is discouraging prayer in tongues. When Paul does remind the Corinthians of the purpose in 14:22, he takes his readers back to prophecy, as did Peter in Acts 2. It is noteworthy that the example[321] has to do with the revelation of God's message, and not at all with prayer. Paul's reminder is consistent with Peter's explanation from Acts 2, and offers nothing that would expand tongues to a broader function. Again, in this context, expansion of the usage of tongues (to include prayer, for example) is discouraged, not encouraged.

Finally, why does Paul use the Greek term *phone* rather than *glossa* in 14:7-11? This pericope considers the purpose of *sound*, the best translation of the Greek *phone* or *voice*, offering several examples of inanimate objects producing sound, including flute, harp, bugle, etc. The reason for the illustration is given in verse 10: "There are perhaps a great many kinds of sounds[322] in the world and no thing soundless."[323] That last word could be translated as *without meaning*. In other words, sounds have distinctness and are recognizable for what they are. If the sound is not recognizable, then how will anyone respond properly to the sound? Leading up to Paul's reminder of the importance of the purpose for tongues, Paul actually

---

[321] Is 28:11-12.
[322] Greek, *phonen*.
[323] Greek, *aphonos*.

discourages the unrecognizable use of tongues *again*. For Paul it is common sense that tongues should be used in its recognizable way.

Is it possible that the Corinthians were using tongues as a prayer language? Not only was it possible, but that seems to be exactly what they were doing. At every turn, Paul discourages – if not prohibits – this unrecognizable use of tongues, because it is not consistent with God's design or purpose. Ironically, the chapter most often cited to try to support tongues as something other than a revelatory gift for purposes of a sign is the one chapter that repeatedly discourages any other usage.

20

Does God Speak to Us Today?

As believers there are certain principles to which we must be thoroughly committed. For example, our experience cannot determine our theology. Instead, we must submit our experience and our theology to God's word. Peter illustrates this principle for us when he explains that even though he had witnessed Christ in His glory at the transfiguration,[324] the prophetic word regarding Christ – or God's revelation – confirmed the issue.[325]

What Peter says on this subject is important, because even if God did presently use experiential or sensory means, it would be secondary to His word. Peter also describes in those verses how God spoke to people – the Holy Spirit moved men to speak the word of God.[326] Certainly, God did speak to people in dreams and other ways.[327] And Paul agrees that all Scripture is God-breathed.[328] Still, in 1 Corinthians 13 Paul describes how the confirming gifts of tongues, prophecy, and knowledge

---

[324] Mt 16:28-17:2; 2 Pet 1:16-18.
[325] 2 Pet 1:19-21.
[326] 2 Pet 1:21.
[327] E.g., Heb 1:1.
[328] 2 Tim 3:16-17.

– gifts whereby God spoke to people – would fulfill their purpose and come to a conclusion.

In a context describing the superiority of love,[329] Paul explains that the gift of tongues would cease on its own.[330] Tongues was a gift which enabled people to speak God's word in actual languages that the speaker didn't understand. This is illustrated in Acts 2:9-11, a passage which includes a list of at least sixteen different languages or dialects by which God used the disciples (and those who were with them) to proclaim God's gospel.

This gift served as a sign to unbelievers,[331] to show that God had sent His Holy Spirit.[332] Paul rebuked the Corinthian church for not utilizing the gift properly at times, and challenged them regarding the importance of love. After that commentary in 1 Corinthians, written in about 51 AD, the Bible never mentions the gift of tongues again – not even in the letter Paul wrote to that same church just a few months later. Very early in church history, the gift of tongues had fulfilled its purpose and ceased on its own, just as Paul indicated it would.

Partial prophecy and knowledge,[333] on the other hand, would continue until the *complete* would arrive,[334] at which time the partial – or incomplete – would be ended. Considering the Greek terminology and syntax of 13:9-10, the issue is not that prophecy and knowledge

---

[329] 1 Cor 13:1-13.
[330] 13:8.
[331] 1 Cor 14:22.
[332] Acts 2:36-38, 10:45-46, 19:5-6.
[333] 1 Cor 13:9.
[334] 13:10.

would be fulfilled by the coming of the complete,[335] but rather that partial[336] prophecy and knowledge would be ended by it. The simplest understanding of these comments by Paul, is that there would come a time when God's revealing through prophecy and words of knowledge would come to a conclusion – that He would have said all He had to say. It is evident that milestone is achieved at the conclusion of the book of Revelation, when Jesus leaves the reader expecting no further communication from God, and with only the remaining exception of the two prophets of Revelation 11, until the return of Christ.[337]

Hebrews 1:1-2 tells us that while God used many methods in former times to communicate, in these last days, He "has spoken to us in His Son." Jesus prepared His disciples for His ascension, telling them the Holy Spirit would come to guide them into all the truth.[338] Upon His departure, He reminded them to "make disciples…teaching them to observe all that I commanded you."[339] The Holy Spirit fulfilled that ministry of guiding the disciples into all the truth, as Peter says, "men moved by the Holy Spirit spoke from God."[340] Jesus' communication, through the Holy Spirit to His disciples, was finished at the end of the book of Revelation.

So, does God speak to us today? Can we interpret dreams or other experiences as His revelations to us?

---

[335] Greek, *to telion*.
[336] Greek, *ek merous*.
[337] Rev 22:18-20.
[338] Jn 16:13-14.
[339] Mt 28:20.
[340] 2 Pet 1:21.

Simple answers: no, and no. We have to understand where we fit in the chronology of God's unfolding plan. There were times when God used dreams to reveal His plans,[341] but as the above passages describe, He simply doesn't utilize those methods right now to speak to His people. That is not to say that He can't use dreams or other experiences to spur us to thought or even possibly to draw our attention to His word – certainly He uses many circumstances in our lives to encourage, nudge or even redirect us. But God has spoken, and His word is the only thing of which we can be certain. As 2 Timothy 3:16-17 says, all Scripture is God-breathed, and useful to equip us for every good work.

So, how do we know what God would have us do in areas that His word hasn't specifically addressed? For example, a believer may wonder if he or she should move from one vocation to another. Gideon had a fleece. Hezekiah had shadows. But what do believers have in order to give us confidence in the Lord's direction? How can a believer know God's will for his or her life when the Bible doesn't specifically address it?

James 1:5 tells us if we are going through difficulty and we don't know how to handle it, that we should ask Him for wisdom, believing in Him, and He will provide it. That means if we are focused on Him as He prescribes, He will give us what we need in order to maneuver the challenges of life. Not by some mystical revelation, but by provision of wisdom so that we can make sound decisions.

---

[341] E.g., as in Dan 2, etc.

Also, Psalm 37:4 is an encouraging and liberating passage: "Delight yourself in the Lord; and He will give you the desires of your heart." If we are taking pleasure in Him, then what our heart wants will align with what He wants. When making difficult decisions, we can simply pursue His glory,[342] ask Him for wisdom believing He will provide,[343] and delight in Him.[344] We can make the tough decision and trust Him with the outcome. He provides confidence, peace, and direction, if we will but listen to what He has already said and has already provided. So we can stop asking Him to repeat Himself, and we can simply take Him at His word.

---

[342] 1 Cor 10:31.
[343] Jam 1:5.
[344] Ps 37:4.

21

Does God Still Heal?

Even if the spiritual gift of healing mentioned in 1 Corinthians 12:9 is no longer in effect in the church, it is still entirely possible that God can, in His mercy, grant *the prayer* of an individual to heal another. Let's say, for example, that there is a sick child in a local church, and the parents call the elders of the church and ask them to pray for the child. The elders come, and pray for the child. Is it possible that God can immediately heal the child? Of course. If He did, would that mean the elders had the gift of healing? No. What's the difference? The Biblical gifts related to signs, miracles, and wonders were granted for a short time in order *to confirm God's message and messenger.*

In other words, with respect to the gift of healing, certain people were given the *authority* to heal others for a specific purpose.[345] In other cases, where the gift was not in play, there is direction to "pray for one another so that you may be healed."[346] With no sign in view, this is just a matter of everyday life in the church. Sometimes we get sick or are weak and need help. Sometimes He heals. Sometimes He doesn't. In the same way, even

---

[345] E.g., Acts 3:6-8.
[346] Jam 5:16.

Elijah had no unique authority over the rain, but by God granting his prayer, the rain stopped for three and a half years.[347]

If God wishes for a people to hear the Gospel in their own language, or if He wishes for a person to be healed, He has the divine right as Creator to do those things, and even to use people to be administrators of those things, if He so desires. *However, for an individual to claim that a specific spiritual gift is in play goes beyond the text*, and puts a person in danger of misdiagnosing what God is doing in the situation. We need to be careful not to put the wrong label on what God is doing. Better simply to glorify God for healing someone, rather than to claim a gift of healing. Better to praise God for allowing someone to be healed rather than to claim a gift of healing.

Can God still work miracles of healing or proclamation of His gospel today? Of course He can, but He makes no promise to do so, and the instruction for believers who would seek His miraculous working is *to pray*, not to search out people who have particular spiritual gifts. We pray, trusting Him with the outcome, whether the miraculous is evident or not. We pray. Sometimes He heals, sometimes He doesn't. He knows best. Are we willing to trust Him, or do we need some mystical sign to ease our lack of trust?

---

[347] 1 Kin 17:1 and Jam 5:17.

22

The Significance of the Modern Dream Phenomena

Nabeel Qureshi, author of *Seeking Allah, Finding Jesus*, describes the significance of dreams in Islamic culture, saying,

> In Muslim cultures, generally speaking, people don't see themselves as being able to commune with God. Communion is a very Christian concept and the idea that Christ has torn down the veil — in a lot of cultures the veil is still up. In Islam, for example, people don't expect to have God talk back to them personally, as the Holy Spirit isn't living in them. They ask God for guidance through dreams; that's like the one way that Muslims expect to hear from God.[348]

Qureshi's description is consistent with many stories of

---

[348] Nicola Menzie, "Report: Isis Fighter Who 'Enjoyed' Killing Christians Wants to Follow Jesus After Dreaming of Man in White Who Told Him 'You Are Killing My People,'" http://www.christianpost.com/news/report-isis-fighter-who-enjoyed-killing-christians-wants-to-follow-jesus-after-dreaming-of-man-in-white-who-told-him-you-are-killing-my-people-139880/.

Muslims having dreams that lead them to Christ. Franklin Graham sees legitimacy in some of these stories, saying, "I can't explain it...I'm not even going to attempt to explain it. I just tell you, it happens. God is at work in that part of the world in a great way."[349] In light of such accounts, Bob Paulson asks an important question: "What should Christians make of such spectacular stories?"[350] Some are skeptical for various reasons, including concerns about the impact of such experiences on the cessationist understanding of sign gifts. I would suggest, though, that *these occurrences actually have absolutely nothing to do with the cessationism or non-cessationism discussion.*

The stories are typically of unbelievers having dreams that point them to Christ, but spiritual gifts are at work in *believers*, members of the body of Christ by virtue of the baptism of the Holy Spirit – a baptism which every believer has had.[351] These dream events are not spiritual gift events. Spiritual gifts are for the edifying of the body, not for evangelism of unbelievers.[352] Certainly, evangelists were given as gifts to the church, and clearly their purpose was to proclaim the gospel to those who were not part of the church, however these dream events are not happening with evangelists, but rather with those needing to become aware of the good news. In short, these

---

[349] Bob Paulson, "A Move of God in the Muslim World," http://billygraham.org/decision-magazine/september-2014/a-move-of-god-in-the-muslim-world/.
[350] Ibid.
[351] 1 Cor 12:13.
[352] Eph 4:11-12.

dreams are not related to gifts of the Spirit. But if not, then how should we understand them?

One of the Holy Spirit's roles during the church age is to convict the world of sin, righteousness, and judgment.[353] There is no discussion of how He does this, but the fact is that He does. Could He possibly use dreams to accomplish this convicting work?

Dreams are only referenced a few times in the New Testament,[354] and while we see that God revealed Himself using dreams throughout the Old Testament, there is no indication that He does so during the church age. Further, the teaching in 1 Corinthians 13, of the ceasing of the revelatory gifts, would seem to preclude the possibility that dreams today are divine revelation. Instead, it seems more likely that the dreams described by Qureshi and others have more to do with the Spirit's convicting than any revelatory function.

It is especially interesting that these things are taking place in geographic regions and cultures which are generally more accepting of the mystical than is our own. Western culture is rooted in a rationalistic idea, while Eastern cultures are often less rationalistic and more responsive to mystical concepts. It makes sense strategically that God might convict people in those cultures in such a way that is sensitive to their own cultures. In the West it seems that stories of conviction are generally (though not exclusively, of course) more rationally based, and are matters of thinking and understanding. It is worth noting that Paul was sensitive

---
[353] Jn 16:8.
[354] Mt 1:20, 2:12, 13, 19, 22, 27:19, Acts 2:17, and Jude 8.

to culture and utilized rather than ignored it when he had Timothy circumcised,[355] when he didn't have Titus circumcised,[356] and when he worked with Athenian culture rather than condemning it.[357] Perhaps in the same way, the Holy Spirit is convicting people within mystical cultures using dreams – something they would recognize as significant.

It is also important to be aware that cultures with a mystical grounding are more prone to overt demonic activity, so we need to be careful not to simply assume that in every case the Holy Spirit is at work.

One point to consider is that as a strategist, Satan might be more likely to use demonic activity out in the open in mystical cultures where people can be easily influenced by mystical occurrences. Whereas in cultures that are more materialistic or rationalistic, it would be foolish to introduce overt demonic activity – the goal of Satan and his forces is not to get people to believe in Satan, but rather to keep them from believing in Christ. Like Roger "Verbal" Klint once said, "The greatest trick the devil ever pulled was convincing the world he didn't exist."[358] It is to be expected that there would be more apparent spiritual activity in cultures that are more open to spirituality. Consequently, we should be cautious about hasty conclusions that wherever there are mystical experiences God must be working in those instances. In

---

[355] Acts 16:3.
[356] Gal 2:3.
[357] Acts 17:23.
[358] *The Usual Suspects*. Directed by Bryan Singer. Los Angeles, CA: MGM Studios, 1995.

many cases, He might be, but there are also other possibilities.

One person has a dream that points them to Christ, and another has a dream that points them away from Christ. We cannot assume that just because someone had a dream that it was prodding from God, though God may be using dreams for that purpose today. Perhaps it was simply a dream, or perhaps there are other influences at work. Either way, we can be confident that God is not presently giving new revelation through dreams, as He has done in ages past, but we can also be confident that the Holy Spirit does indeed convict the world of sin, righteousness, and judgment, and He is very effective at it. Perhaps the dream phenomena are part of that ministry, or perhaps not. In either case, we praise God that people are being led to Christ, whether through the prodding of dreams or through other ways. And we are cautious to rightly distinguish between the gifts of the Holy Spirit for the church, and His ministry to unbelievers.

134 Gifted

23

The Nature of Prophecy

During Old Testament times, God used many ways to communicate Himself to people,[359] but He especially used prophecy. He commissioned men to whom He would give His word, and whom He would send out to deliver His message. Those men were called prophets, and were recognized as being sent by God. The prophetic standard for accuracy was perfection. If the prophet had not spoken from God and was wrong even once, he was to be considered a false prophet, and the penalty was extreme.[360] Also, even if a prophet was able to work signs, miracles, or wonders, if he wasn't speaking according to God's revealed truth, he was to be rejected as a false prophet.[361]

There were four distinct periods of prophecy during Old Testament times: the foundational era, the kingdom era, the exilic era, and the post-exilic era. The foundational era included Abraham, the first person to be called a prophet,[362] Moses as the second,[363] then Deborah,

---

[359] Heb 1:1.
[360] Deut 18:20-22.
[361] Deut 13:1-5.
[362] Gen 20:7.
[363] Deut 34:10.

the prophetess,[364] Samuel,[365] a group of unnamed prophets,[366] even perhaps Saul – Israel's first king during the kingdom or monarchy era,[367] and then David.[368]

As the era of Israel's kings began, Nathan was an early notable prophet[369] who, along with Gad[370] served during David's rule. Ahijah announced that the kingdom would be divided.[371] There were some unnamed prophets, including two in 1 Kings 13 – one dishonest, the other one honest. Jehu served during the early divided kingdom,[372] along with many others[373] whose names were not mentioned in the Bible. Then we are introduced to Elijah,[374] followed by Elisha,[375] Jonah,[376] Isaiah,[377] Huldah the prophetess,[378] along with several others – Shemaiah and Iddo,[379] Azariah,[380] Oded,[381] and finally, Jeremiah.[382]

---

[364] Judg 4:4.
[365] 1 Sam 3:20.
[366] 1 Sam 10:10.
[367] 1 Sam 10:11-12.
[368] Acts 2:30.
[369] 2 Sam 7:2.
[370] 2 Sam 24:11.
[371] 1 Kin 11:19.
[372] 1 Kin 16:7.
[373] 1 Kin 18:4.
[374] 1 Kin 18:36.
[375] 2 Kin 2:15, 9:1.
[376] 2 Kin 14:25.
[377] 2 Kin 20:1.
[378] 2 Kin 22:14.
[379] 2 Chron 9:15.
[380] 2 Chron 15:8.
[381] 2 Chron 28:9.
[382] 2 Chron 36:12.

The Nature of Prophecy

During this time there were written a number of prophetic books, including some to the nations in general, some to the Northern Kingdom of Israel, and some to the Southern Kingdom of Judah. Jonah, Obadiah, and Nahum prophesied to nations, including Assyria and Edom. Amos and Hosea addressed the Northern Kingdom, specifically. Six prophets presented God's word to the Southern Kingdom: Joel, Micah, Isaiah, Zephaniah, Habbakkuk, and Jeremiah.

The Northern Kingdom was conquered first, in 721 BC, and the Southern Kingdom went into exile between 605 and 586 BC. During the exile period of the Southern Kingdom, Jeremiah wrote Lamentations, and Ezekiel and Daniel also wrote their prophetic books. After the return from exile of the people of Judah to Jerusalem, there were prophets who ministered, including Noadiah the prophetess,[383] and three prophets who wrote – Haggai, Zechariah, and Malachi. Malachi's prophecy closed with the prediction of a forerunner to the Messiah,[384] a prediction that Zacharias (through the Holy Spirit) and Jesus, Himself, identified as being at least partially fulfilled by John.[385]

There was also additional prophetic confirmation of Jesus as the Messiah, including from Anna the prophetess in Luke 2:36-38. Jesus the Messiah was the prophet Moses anticipated.[386] He was recognized as the

---

[383] Neh 6:14.
[384] Mal 3:1, 4:5.
[385] Lk 1:76, Mt 11:9-15.
[386] Deut 18:18.

prophet,[387] and He identified Himself as a prophet.[388] He is the cornerstone of the church, which is built upon the foundation of the apostles and the (New Testament) prophets.

The prophets that followed Jesus during the church age were ministering within and to the church, utilizing gifts of prophecy,[389] to communicate God's word as He determined. But those prophecies were always partial prophecies,[390] as they were parts of a greater whole – the complete revealed word of God.[391] After the church age is complete, God will use two prophets to testify of Him,[392] as the day of the Lord progresses, and as He prepares the world for His coming.

From beginning to end, this is how prophecy is cataloged in the Bible. The question asked by many is where prophecy fits today during the church age. While the answer seems fairly evident, from the above examination, not all agree that prophecy in the church age is finished when the revealed word is complete – or at any time during the early church era. Some suggest that prophecy continues even today.

It is not uncommon to hear of a distinction in kinds of prophecy between foretelling and forthtelling. In this understanding, foretelling is predictive, and forthtelling is proclamation. In this view, foretelling – or prediction – may have run its course, but forthtelling – proclamation

---

[387] Mt 21:11, Lk 7:16, Jn 4:19, Acts 3:22, 7:37.
[388] Mk 6:4.
[389] Rom 12:6.
[390] 1 Cor 13:9.
[391] 1 Cor 13:10.
[392] Rev 11.

– continues today. Stephen McKenzie, for example, draws this type of distinction, which allows him to characterize Martin Luther King Jr. as "a kind of modern day prophet."[393] In this view, prophecy continues today, and is proclamation rather than prediction.

Wayne Grudem goes a step further, saying that, "there certainly were prophets prophesying in many local congregations after the death of the apostles,"[394] but he makes the argument that such prophecies – along with the prophecies of today – "are not 'the words of God.'"[395] He defines prophecy uniquely as, "telling something that God has spontaneously brought to mind."[396] He suggests that "prophecy is a valuable gift...but it is in Scripture that God and only God speaks to us his very words."[397] Grudem's view is that even New Testament prophets can be wrong. He asserts that Agabus' prophecy in Acts 21:10-11, for example, "was not far off, but it had inaccuracies in detail."[398] Essentially, in order to accommodate an ongoing form of prophecy in the church today, Grudem divides prophecy into two categories – the prophecy that was recorded as God's written word, and ongoing prophecy that does not quite have the authority of God's word and can even be wrong at times. But does Biblical exegesis support such a division between kinds of

---

[393] Stephen McKenzie, *How to Read the Bible* (New York, Oxford University Press, 2005), 46, 68-69.
[394] Wayne Grudem, *Systematic Theology* (Grand Rapids, MI: InterVarsity Press, 1994), 1055.
[395] Ibid.
[396] Ibid., 1049.
[397] Ibid., 1061.
[398] Ibid. 1052.

prophecy, or that prophecy continues in the present era of the church? The function and longevity of prophecy are considered in the next chapter.

24

Are Revelatory Gifts for Today?[399]

Introduction

While not the only passage on the topic, 1 Corinthians 13 is a pivotal context on the issue of whether or not the revelatory gifts continue for the church's use today or whether they have ceased. The eighth verse catalogs three particular nouns to highlight their temporality in contrast with the enduring nature of love (*agape*): prophecies (*prophetai*, nominative plural), tongues (*glossai*, nominative plural), and knowledge (*gnosis*, nominative singular).

In this context these three are not explicitly identified as gifts, though 12:4 mentions that there are varieties of gifts (*charisma*). Paul adds that "to each is given a manifestation (*phanerosis*) of the Spirit for the common good" (12:7). Following the designation of "manifestation," Paul refers (in a list that includes other manifestations) to the same three he later addresses in chapter 13. Though his verbiage is slightly different in 12, he mentions word of knowledge (12:8, *logos gnoseos*), prophecy (12:10, *propheteia*), and other kinds of tongues

---

[399] Presented to the SCS Faculty Symposium on the Holy Spirit and Spiritual Gifts, Southern California Seminary, El Cajon, California, July 27, 2015.

(12:10, *hetero gene glosson*), along with a second category related to tongues, the interpretation of tongues (*hermeneia glosson*).

These three manifestations share the common trait of communicating aspects of God's revelation. Prophecy is directly identified as a vehicle for revelation (2 Pet 1:20-21), while word of knowledge would seem at least closely related to revelation, since it was given and not learned (1 Cor 12:8). Tongues, though serving as a sign to unbelievers (1 Cor 14:22), was nonetheless also a content-oriented manifestation. The function of tongues was to communicate God's truth in languages the speaker had not learned (e.g., Acts 2:4-6).

Paul adds two hypothetical functions for tongues, including speaking with the tongues of angels (1 Cor 13:1), and praying in tongues (14:14). But nowhere does he advocate for the actuality of these two, so we have no reason to think they were anything other than hyperbole. Notice in 1 Corinthians 13:3, Paul discusses the giving of all his possessions to feed the poor and the presenting of his body to be burned as hypothetical, and there is no indication that he actually did these two things. So if tongues was not a method of communicating with angels, nor a legitimate means of prayer, then its only demonstrable function is the one evidenced in Acts 2 – the communication of God's word, specifically relaying the mighty deeds of God (2:11).

While Peter does not describe the Pentecost tongues event as a fulfillment of Joel 2:28-29, he identified the two contexts as related, in that they both evidenced the outpouring of the Holy Spirit, and their results included a prophetic component (2:18). In so doing, it seems that Peter recognizes a revelatory aspect to the manifestation of tongues. If this is so, then all three of the gifts Paul discusses in 1 Corinthians 13:8-13 are revelatory in nature, and it is appropriate to recognize a contrast between the eternality of love and the temporality of the revelatory manifestations (or gifts). Consequently, revelatory manifestations were never expected to be anything but short lived. The question at issue here is just how short lived they would be. Would they cease at the second coming of Christ, or at the maturing of the church, or at the inauguration of the eternal state, or at the completion of God's revealed word? There is no question that these revelatory manifestations would cease at some point. The question of timing is addressed here.

The Cessation of the Three Revelatory Functions

Paul describes the conclusion and fulfillment of the revelatory sign gifts in 1 Corinthians 13:10, when he says, "but when the perfect comes, the partial will be done away." The perfect is *to teleion*, and is translated in different contexts as perfect, genuine, complete, mature, adult, or even initiated. How this word is translated in 13:10 is the most significant lexical issue regarding miraculous sign gifts. If in this context it is best translated mature or adult, then Paul's implication would be that sign gifts are done away as a maturing (either individual or corporate) occurs. If it is best translated perfect, then it would seem most likely that Paul is referencing some aspect of the eternal state or even the return of Christ (as that which initiates perfection). If the intended meaning of *to teleion* is the complete, or that which is completed, then in this context of sign gifts which are all related to revelation, it would seem a certain reference to God's complete revelation – a completed Scripture – even if not yet at that point of completion fully recognized as canonical.

In 13:8, there are three revelatory sign gifts or functions (they are not specifically referred to as gifts in this context) mentioned: prophecy, tongues, and knowledge. Prophecy and knowledge both end the same way: they are done away – prophecies, in the plural (*katargethesontai*) and knowledge, in the singular (*katargethesetai*). The verb, *katergeo* (to put an end to or stop to) in both cases is passive voice, meaning that an outside force will end these abruptly. Tongues, on the other hand, will cease (*pausontai*). This verb is in the middle voice, meaning that the subject is acting upon itself: tongues will cease themselves. Tongues is the first of these three to go. Remember the contrast: love never fails, but these other three will. Verses 9-10 discuss a specific event that brings the "failing" or limitation of prophecy and knowledge, but by the time that event happens, tongues have already ceased themselves. Tongues are the least significant of these three revelatory sign gifts or functions. Remember that after the mentions of tongues in 1 Corinthians 12-14 tongues is never again mentioned during the remaining forty or so years of New Testament history – not once.

In 13:9, Paul identifies the particular kind of prophecy and knowledge that will be done away: "For we know in part and we prophesy in part." Literally translated, *ek merous*, is in or from a part. It is not that prophecy and knowledge will disappear, it is that *partial* prophecy and knowledge will be done away. Paul says "we know...and prophesy..." – both verbs are present active indicative. The prophesying and knowledge that was presently in effect during Paul's day was in part. In extolling love's superiority, Paul identifies in 13:10 the event that will end partial knowledge and partial prophecy: "but when the perfect comes, the partial will be done away." The NASB, KJV, and ESV all translate *to teleion* as "the perfect." The NetBible translates the same way, but adds the appropriate note, "Or 'when completion'." The word *teleios* can have any one of several meanings, but when Paul has just established the antonym as partial in the previous verse, the natural reading of the text would be to translate *teleios* as complete, rather than perfect. Paul is not contrasting imperfect and perfect. He is contrasting partial and complete. That contrast governs the illustrations to follow – they do not govern the contrast.

The Examples

For example, in 13:11 Paul illustrates that there is a difference between the speech, thoughts, and reasonings of a child and those of a man. From this example, some conclude that Paul's contrast in 13:9-10 is of immature and mature, but *merous* is never used elsewhere to reference immaturity (especially note Paul's uses in 1 Cor 12:27 and in Eph 4:16). Paul employs the illustration to show that childish things are partial, and unfitting for an adult. He introduces the idea of logical progression. This doing away of prophecy and knowledge is part of a logical progression, and it is the coming of the complete that brings it about.

Likewise, 13:12 provides another example – this one illustrates clarity of focus or certainty. "For we now see in a mirror dimly, but then face to face..." The term translated mirror (*esoptrou*) is used only one other time in the NT. In James 1:23 the term is used in the context of illustrating that one who looks at the word but is not a doer of it is like one who looks in a mirror and forgets his face. In both instances, the near-context referent is the word of God and human response to it. In 1 Cor 13:12, the mirror is engaged *en ainigmati* – in a dim (or enigmatic) image, but then "face to face." Because of this latter phrase, some suggest *to teleion* references the eternal state (after all, we will be face to face with Jesus, right?). And I certainly admit that this phrase is difficult to justify with the contrast of partial versus complete. However, even with this difficulty, we must prioritize either a phrase in a secondary illustration or we must prioritize the primary contrast undergirding the entire context: partial versus complete. I prioritize the latter, and consider the former simply one of many Pauline mixed metaphors (e.g., as in 1 Cor 3:1-17).

"Now I know in part." Again, *ek merous*, from a part. "But then I will know fully..." This phrase is translated in such a way that we might infer the eternal state is in view. For when else will we know fully? But it does not say we will know fully. The word translated know fully is *epignosomai*, and it simply means to understand or to have certainty. Romans 3:20 uses the same root word to describe the present knowledge of sin brought by law. The eternal state is not in view here. "Just as I also have been fully known." This phrase uses the same verb as in the earlier phrase – not fully known, but rather, understood or recognized. Either way, the contrast is to *ek merous*, and that is probably why the verb is translated as *fully known*.

We should admit that worthy arguments could be mounted for both of these Pauline illustrations (the child/man and mirror/face to face) as portraying the maturing of the church, the eternal state, or the completed Scriptures. It should also be recognized that none of these examples provide conclusive arguments in themselves. But ultimately Paul employs these examples to illustrate his earlier primary contrast – partial versus complete.

In any case, partial prophecy and knowledge will be done away as revelatory vehicles, because the complete will have arrived. The natural reading of this context favors the completed revelation of God as taking the place of the partial, and hence the vehicles for partial knowledge and revelation are simply no longer needed, having fully served their revelatory purpose.

If we would argue that this is *not* what Paul intended to communicate, then we must address three major resulting difficulties: (1) the exegetical one, in which we must discard *ek merous* and *to teleion* as contrasting ideas altogether, (2) the theological one, in which there is absolutely no need or justification for a completed written revelation at all [if this is the case how can Rev 22:18-19 prohibit additions and subtractions, when theoretically, additions, at least, should be possible?], and (3) the historical one, in which if tongues, prophecy, and knowledge endure, we should expect them to be fairly common if not normative in the church, yet even in the seminal apostolic age of the church, tongues, for example, receives no mention beyond AD 54.

What About Modern Manifestations?

Alleged modern manifestations of tongues do not fit the characteristics of tongues as it is described in these passages – either in substance or in function. It has been argued here that tongues – the revelatory sign gift described and discussed in Acts and 1 Corinthians – has been fulfilled and is no longer in play in the church. But if that argument is true, is it possible that someone today can speak the Gospel in a tongue or language they have not learned? Certainly, it is possible. But such an occurrence *would not fit the parameters of the Biblical gift of tongues.* The Biblical gift of tongues was intended both as a sign and as a vehicle for divine revelation. If God's revelation is complete, then tongues, if still in play, could have no further revealing function – which was a major component of their purpose.

Does Revelation 11 Argue Against Cessationism of Revelatory Functions?

The context of 1 Corinthians 12-14 considers three kinds of manifestations of the Spirit (12:7) in the body of Christ: gifts, ministries, and effects. Paul's larger point is that these are all given for the common good (12:7), and that without love they cannot achieve their purpose (13:1-3). Love and the building up of the body is the point. The listed manifestations of the Spirit are significant means to that end. The key point as it relates to this particular question is that the manifestation of the Spirit is given (hence the loose references to the manifestations as gifts) within and for the body of Christ. The context for spiritual gifts is exclusively the body of Christ. Consequently, the idea that the completed written revelation does away with prophecy needs to be slightly qualified: *it does away with prophecy as a partial-revelation spiritual manifestation or gift in the church.* Paul is not discussing prophecy outside of that context. What we see in Revelation 11 is a different context altogether.

The two witnesses are indeed prophesying (Rev 11:3), and are even dealing in the realm of signs and miracles (11:6). But it is very notable that their ministry is a testimony (11:7) to the peoples, tribes, and tongues (11:9), and is considered by the people on earth to be torment, not edification (11:10). The church is no longer on earth, not having been specifically referenced after Revelation 3, and the church won't return to the earth until Christ does in Revelation 19:11. In short, the two witnesses are not church-age believers, they are not ministering to the church, and they are not utilizing spiritual manifestations or gifts as Paul described them. The ministry of the two witnesses is more like the Hebrew prophets of Israel's monarchy period than anything we see during the church age.

The completed written revelation doesn't end prophecy as a tool in God's toolbox for use after the church age, but it does end prophecy as a partial-revelation spiritual manifestation or gift to the church.

25

Eternal Security, The Holy Spirit, And Biblical Ethics

Practice is *from* position, but never *to* position. The ethical mandates of the New Testament are decisively clear that believers are to walk in the richness of the position we have been given,[400] and that the position is actually necessary for the walk.[401] Never is a believer warned that his or her position as a child of God is in danger because of their walk. Certainly there are warning passages. Hebrews 4:1 warns us to fear lest we "may seem to have come short" of entering His rest. Hebrews 4:11 prescribes diligence so that "no one will fall." In the same context, the writer exhorts, "let us draw near with confidence to the throne of grace, so that we may receive mercy and find grace to help in time of need."[402] Why else would we need continuing grace and mercy if we were without sin in our practice?

Later, the writer reminds, "we are not of those who shrink back to destruction.[403] There is no future of

---

[400] Eph 1:3.
[401] Heb 11:6.
[402] Heb 4:16.
[403] Heb 10:39.

destruction for believers because "the believing one has eternal life."[404] Once eternal life is given, then by definition, it is eternal. Any end to it would make it something other than eternal. The warnings, then, are not about loss of position, but about loss within that position. One whose practice is lacking will suffer loss – even losing reward – but that person is still secure in position.[405]

The Corinthians illustrate well how position should lead to a certain kind of walk but doesn't always. Paul chastises them for being fleshly,[406] as they engaged in severe immorality.[407] He challenges them to stop behaving immaturely like those who have not been transferred to the kingdom of God,[408] and instead to have maturity in their thinking.[409] Some of the Corinthians were exceedingly guilty in their practice, but all of them had been washed, sanctified, and justified.[410]

Another key evidence for the positional security of the believer is the work of the Holy Spirit. The Holy Spirit enables believers to walk well, and He indwells every believer as the guarantee of eternal life.[411] He baptized every believer into the body of Christ.[412] Every believer has Him,[413] and He is the source of fruitbearing in the

---

[404] Jn 6:47.
[405] 1 Cor 3:12-15.
[406] 1 Cor 3:1.
[407] 1 Cor 5:1.
[408] 1 Cor 6:9-10, Col 1:13.
[409] 1 Cor 14:20.
[410] 1 Cor 6:11.
[411] Eph 1:13-14.
[412] 1 Cor 12:13.
[413] Rom 8:9.

lives of all believers.[414] Certainly, one's deeds can provide an evidence of position, but even when our deeds seem to be contrary, the witness of the Holy Spirit remains true.[415] Our source of assurance is not our deeds, but the Holy Spirit Who lives within us.

Further, notice how the Biblical writers motivate based on position: "Therefore I urge you, brethren, by the mercies of God, to present your bodies a living and holy sacrifice, acceptable to God, which is your spiritual service of worship."[416] "Therefore I, the prisoner of the Lord, implore you to walk in a manner worthy of the calling with which you have been called..."[417] "Therefore leaving the elementary teaching about the Christ, let us press on to maturity, not laying again a foundation of repentance from dead works and of faith toward God..."[418] "Are you so foolish? Having begun by the Spirit, are you now being perfected by the flesh?[419] "Therefore the Law has become our tutor to lead us to Christ, so that we may be justified by faith. But now that faith has come, we are no longer under a tutor."[420] "Therefore if you have been raised up with Christ, keep seeking the things above, where Christ is, seated at the right hand of God. Set your mind on the things above, not on the things that are on earth. For you have died and your life is hidden with Christ in God. When Christ, who is our life, is revealed,

---

[414] Gal 5:22.
[415] 1 Jn 4:13.
[416] Rom 12:1.
[417] Eph 4:1.
[418] Heb 6:1.
[419] Gal 3:3.
[420] Gal 3:24-25.

then you also will be revealed with Him in glory. Therefore consider the members of your earthly body as dead to immorality, impurity, passion, evil desire, and greed, which amounts to idolatry."[421] "Blessed be the God and Father of our Lord Jesus Christ, who according to His great mercy has caused us to be born again to a living hope through the resurrection of Jesus Christ from the dead, to obtain an inheritance which is imperishable and undefiled and will not fade away, reserved in heaven for you, who are protected by the power of God through faith for a salvation ready to be revealed in the last time."[422]

Biblical ethics are based not on fear of losing one's position as a child of God or as a member of the body of Christ. Instead, one's position is the platform from which they should practice. It is the joyous new beginning from which we can honor God, having been redeemed and cleansed. Sadly, it is not uncommon for us as believers to sin against God – even in some horrific ways. In this we must know that we should not continue in sin so that grace can increase.[423] We are told straightforwardly that we are not to let sin rule over our bodies,[424] and that grace is not a license to sin.[425] In fact, Paul explains that for a person who has died to sin – as all believers have – to continue in sin is an utterly ridiculous proposition.[426] It is nonsense, but still possible. Instead, we should consider

---

[421] Col 3:1-5.
[422] 1 Pet 1:3-5.
[423] Rom 6:1-2.
[424] Rom 6:12, 14.
[425] Rom 6:15.
[426] Rom 6:2.

God's mercies, and present our bodies to Him – that is reasonable.[427]

---

[427] Rom 12:1.

26

How Shall We Then Live? The Christian's Constant Choice Between Two Paths

In a section of Paul's Letter to the Galatians explaining how Christians should handle the freedom they have in Christ, there is a very practical contrast of two modes of life: walking by the Spirit and walking according to the flesh. Paul introduces the contrast in 2:20, when he says "I have been crucified with Christ; and it is no longer I who live, but Christ in me; and the life I live in the flesh I live by faith in the Son of God and gave Himself up for me." There is more to life here than simply living in the flesh.

He questions in 3:3, "Are you so foolish? Having begun by the Spirit are you now being perfected by the flesh? The Galatian believers were falling into an error regarding their daily walk with God. They had rightly come to be saved by grace through faith, and were thus regenerated by the Holy Spirit, but they were walking as if their growth would come simply from external obedience to rules and regulations. Specifically, some were trying to place themselves under elements of the Mosaic Law, so that they could meet a standard that was just a little higher than the standard of others. Even for those (in earlier generations) who actually lived under Mosaic Law, their salvation was not through obedience to the Law.

In Matthew 5-7 Jesus explains that righteousness comes not from external obedience, but is demonstrated by internal character (which of course, we might expect to have an effect on external behavior). This was one reason the Law couldn't save anyone: it was only a measuring stick to show the need for the righteousness that comes through redemption.[428]

Those Galatians, then, that had fallen into a legalistic approach to their walk, and were not walking according to the Spirit, but were instead depending on their own flesh. Just as Paul illustrated from his own life so vividly in Romans 7, for the Christian, there is a battle between the spirit within them and their flesh. He explains in Galatians 5:17 that "the flesh sets its desire against the Spirit, and the Spirit against the flesh." In Romans 7, Paul contrasts the flesh with the believer's own spirit, while in Galatians 5, the Spirit he is talking about is the Holy Spirit, and not just the newly alive spirit within us (see Gal 3:2, 14, 6:8). So Paul presents a model for Christian living: if we depend on ourselves, we will not walk properly. But if we depend on God (specifically, the Holy Spirit who indwells us), then we can walk properly.

The contrasting walks are identified in 5:16 – walk by the Spirit, or carry out the desire of the flesh. These

---

[428] Gal 3:24.

How Shall We Then Live? 159

two are in opposition to one another, are not compatible, and ultimately have diametrically opposing results.[429] The deeds of the flesh include a laundry list of dirty laundry: immorality, impurity, sensuality, idolatry, sorcery, enmity, strife, jealousy, outbursts of anger, disputes dissensions, factions, envying, drunkenness, carousing, and things like these..."[430] Just in case anyone can't figure out that these are bad things, Paul reminds the readers that these are the natural outworkings of those who are not transferred to God's kingdom.[431] So how ridiculous would it be for believers – who have been reborn and transferred to His kingdom above – to behave as those who are dead in their sins,[432] and as those who are not sealed by the Holy Spirit,[433] and as those who do not have the Holy Spirit dwelling in them?[434]

Instead of fleshly deeds, the Holy Spirit bears fruit in the believer: love, joy, peace, patience, kindness, goodness, faithfulness, gentleness, and self-control.[435] But the believer has a responsibility to *walk by the Spirit*.[436] In 5:16 the term walk is the imperative form of the Greek *peripateo* – meaning *walk around*. In 5:25 the term translated as walk is *stoichomen* – which means *to conduct oneself, or to go about the course of life*. Notice Paul's play on words in 5:25 – if we live (have our

---

[429] Gal 5:17.
[430] Gal 5:19-21.
[431] As in Col 1:13.
[432] As in Eph 2:1-4.
[433] Eph 1:13-14.
[434] Rom 8:9.
[435] Gal 5:22-23.
[436] Gal 5:16,25.

existence) by the Spirit, then we should live (conduct ourselves) by the Spirit. It's kind of a *dance with the one that brung ya* concept.

As Christians, we have new life through Christ, being now children of the Father, and indwelt by the Holy Spirit. Positionally we have been given this incredible spiritual wealth,[437] and now, as Paul put it, we need to walk in a manner worthy of that calling.[438] Our practice should fit our position. If our practice doesn't fit our position, it doesn't change our position, but it creates an absurdity in the life of the believer. As Paul asks in Galatians 3:3, "are you so foolish? Having begun by the Spirit are you being perfected (or completed) by the flesh?"

How then do we walk by the Spirit? Paul emphasizes to the Galatians that they should walk in the same way they received their position – *hearing with faith*.[439] Ultimately what was heard was the word of God.[440] We come to know Him and be reborn by hearing the word of God with faith in Him.[441] That word is also called the sword of the Spirit,[442] and is authored by the Holy Spirit.[443] As Paul illustrates in Ephesians 5:18, the believer should be filled or controlled by the Holy Spirit, and that happens when we are pouring His word into us, and are submitting to it – hearing God's word, and

---

[437] Eph 1:3.
[438] Eph 4:1.
[439] Gal 3:2.
[440] Gal 3:5-14.
[441] As in Rom 10:17, Jn 3:16, etc.
[442] Eph 6:17.
[443] 2 Pet 1:20-21.

responding in faith. Paul describes this elsewhere as "being transformed by the renewing of your mind,"[444] and explains that in that process we are proving what the will of God is[445] – that which is good, acceptable, and perfect.

So we have a choice at every moment. Will we walk by the Spirit as people who are hearing with faith? Or will we walk by the flesh, depending on our own strength and following our own desires? This is a choice that every Christian faces at every moment.

---

[444] Rom 12:2.
[445] Just like as in Eph 5:17.

Epilogue

The Importance of How We Interpret the Bible[446]

We owe a tremendous debt to many who labored to blaze trails more Biblical than those of their forefathers. Still, we must continue to refine for an increasingly *more Biblical* understanding. To that end, this chapter has three concerns.

First, it explores dispensationalism's concurrent dissatisfaction with non–literal eschatology and contentment with thomistic and reformed (hereafter, TR) platforms in soteriology and ecclesiology. Due to historical sympathy toward these platforms, we have failed to fully deconstruct our theology and reconstruct from a hermeneutically sound Biblical perspective. Consequently, our systematic theology is not univocally systematic or Biblical, but rather is an amalgamation of broadly informed historical systems.

Second, as such amalgamations eventually breaks down in favor of one system over another, we are not

---

[446] Presented to the Council on Dispensational Hermeneutics, Clarks Summit, Pennsylvania, September 18-19, 2013 as "Dispensationalism's Feet of Iron Mixed With Clay: How We Arrived at an Open-but-Cautious View."

surprised in soteriology to see a settling in the lordship salvation debate, for example, as illustrated by the increasing prominence of the Young Restless, and Reformed, and the New Calvinists. Likewise, in evangelical ecclesiology there is an increasing drift toward an open but cautious view on non-cessationism, fostered in part by shared methodology of MacArthur and Piper on the issue.

Finally, as a remedy to drift favoring TR methodology and conclusions, we propose a full deconstruction of dispensational theology, and a reconstruction *in order* on literal grammatical–historical principles. If dispensationalism is to have any true explanatory value, it must fully extricate itself from the systems it has concurrently espoused and eschewed.

Argument in Brief

The primary (inductive) argument of this paper is presented here in short form:

> *P1: Dispensationalism has historically disagreed with fundamental aspects of TR ecclesiology and eschatology.*
>
> *P2: The explanation for the differences, according to representatives of each group, is centrally theological and hermeneutical.*
>
> *P3: Dispensationalism has historically agreed with fundamental aspects of TR soteriology, while*

disagreeing on some points (as illustrated by Chafer).

P4: An explanation for the soteriological similarities is found centrally in the shared methodology of appealing to TR authorities (as illustrated by MacArthur and Piper).

P5: TR methodology is compatible with an open but cautious view on non-cessationism.

C: As long as dispensationalism appeals to TR methodology for any of its doctrines, inconsistencies identifiable in TR eschatology and soterology will be present within dispensational thought. With respect to the cessationism debate, this means dispensationalism will have increasing difficulty in arguing against non-cessationism unless it abandons TR methodology altogether.

Argument

Premise1: Dispensationalism has historically disagreed with fundamental aspects of TR ecclesiology and eschatology.

While this disagreement is common knowledge, the historical differences relating to Israel's present and future are worth noting here. Ronald Diprose observes, "Christian theology should consider Israel for her own sake and not as an adjunct to a particular theological system."[447] Diprose notes that there are a number of passages viewed by some as being compatible with replacement theology, including John 8:30-59; Matthew 21:42-44; Acts 15:1-18; Galatians 3:26-29, 6:16; Ephesians 2:11-22; Hebrews 8:1-13; 1 Peter 2:4-10; Philippians 3:4-9, and 1 Thessalonians 2:15-16.[448] (I would also add Revelation 20:1-10 as a central passage in the discussion.) How these particular passages are handled goes a long way in determining ecclesiology and eschatology. While there are several permutations of supersessionist thought,[449] the purpose here is not to explicate them all, but only to show a central point of contrast between dispensational and TR thought in this area.

Diprose traces early strands of replacement theology from the Epistle of Barnabas, where it is said, "But let us see whether this people is the heir or the former, and if the covenant belongs to them or to us."[450] Justin Martyr considered the church to be the true Israelitish race,[451] Diprose further catalogs how Iranaeus, Tertullian, Origen, Ambrose, Augustine, Chrysostom, Cyril, Pope Gregory I, Constantine, and subsequent canon law all were influential in swaying the church toward a predominantly supersessionist perspective.[452]

---

[447] Ronald Diprose, *Israel and the Church* (Waynesboro, GA: authentic Media, 2004), 3.
[448] Diprose, 33-54.
[449] The distinct systems are well cataloged by Michael Vlach in "Various Forms of Replacement Theology" in *The Masters Seminary Journal* 20:1 (Spring, 2009): 57-69.
[450] Diprose, 73.
[451] Diprose, 75.
[452] Diprose, 77-96.

Thomas Aquinas later solidifies supersessionism, commenting on Galatians 6:16 that, "He therefore is the Israel of God who is spiritually an Israel before God...Hence even the Gentiles have become the Israel of God..."[453] Martin Luther, in his commentary on Galatians makes no direct distinction between Israel and the church, nor does he equate the two.[454] However, an editorial comment in Luther's *Commentary on Romans* illustrates Luther's wrestling and final resolution on the identity of Israel in Romans 11:

> Luther at first wavered with regard to the conversion of "all Israel." In Romans he at times speaks as though he believed in the final conversion of the Jews, though he also emphasizes the fact that only the elect will be saved. Later he definitely accepted the opinion of Origen, Theophylact, Jerome, and others, who identified "all Israel" with the number of the elect, to which corresponds the expression "the fullness of the Gentiles.[455]

---

[453] Thomas Aquinas, *Commentary on the Epistle to the Galatians*, trans. F.R. Larcher, OP (Albany, NY: Magi Books, 1966), electronic edition.
[454] Martin Luther, *Commentary on St. Paul's Epistle to the Galatians* (Grand Rapids, MI: CCEL, 1991), 135.
[455] Martin Luther, *Commentary on Romans*, trans. Peter Miller (Grand Rapids, MI: Zondervan, 1954), 162.

John Calvin adds, citing Galatians 6:15, that, "The Old Testament has reference to one nation, the New to all nations."[456] Commenting on 6:16, he suggests that

> There are two classes that bear [Abraham's] name, a pretended Israel, which appears to be so in the sight of men, – and the Israel of God. Circumcision was a disguise before men, but regeneration is a truth before God. In a word, he gives the appellation of the Israel of God, to those whom he formerly denominated the children of Abraham by faith (Galatians 3:29), and thus includes all believers, whether Jews of Gentiles, who were united into one church.[457]

Aquinas, Luther, and Calvin illustrate, by their exposition, a common strand of basic supersessionism that has come to dominate church history, yet which is contradicted in premillennial and especially dispensational thought.

Premise 2: The explanation for the differences, according to representatives of each group, is centrally theological and hermeneutical.

Unlike the TR approach, John Darby notes that the Israel of God referred to "any of that people [Israel] who were circumcised in heart, who gloried in the cross

---

[456] John Calvin, *Institutes of the Christian Religion*, trans. Ford Battles (Philadelphia, PA: Westminster Press, 1940), 2:11:11.
[457] John Calvin, *Commentary on Galatians and Ephesians*, trans. William Pringle (Grand Rapids, MI: CCEL), 154.

Epilogue: The Importance of How We Interpret the Bible 169

according to the sentiments of the new creature."[458] Darby was careful to maintain the ethnic distinction, though he does add, with reference to *them* in 6:16, "Moreover every true Christian was of them according to the spirit of his walk."[459]

While Charles Ryrie admits that grammar is not dispositive in Galatians 6:16, for example,[460] he carefully exposits:

> The argument of the book of Galatians does favor the connective or emphatic meaning of "and"...Use of the words Israel and Church shows clearly that in the New Testament national Israel continues with her own promises and the Church is never equated with a so-called "new Israel" but is carefully and continually distinguished as a separate work of God in this age.[461]

S. Lewis Johnson agrees, and underscores a major issue encountered in the TR interpretation of the *kai* as explicative:

> If there is an interpretation that totters on a tenuous foundation, it is the view that Paul equates the term "the Israel of God" with the believing church of Jews and Gentiles. To support

---

[458] J.N. Darby, *Synopsis of the Books of the Bible, Vol. IV* (London, England: Cooper and Budd, Ltd., 1965), 281.
[459] Darby, 281.
[460] Charles Ryrie, *Dispensationalism Today* (Chicago, IL: Moody Press, 1965), 139.
[461] Ryrie, 140.

it, the general usage of the term Israel in Paul, in the NT, and in the Scriptures as a whole is ignored.[462]

What Johnson observes is that in order for some to favor a particular theological conclusion, characteristics of common usage are not properly appreciated. The TR interpretation, though driven by presuppositions, employs different methodology than that used to derive the dispensational understanding.

Oswald T. Allis observes, "One of the most marked features of Premillennialism in all its forms is the emphasis which it places on the literal interpretation of Scripture. It is the insistent claim of its advocates that only when interpreted literally is the Bible interpreted truly."[463] He recognizes that dispensationalists "are literalists in interpreting prophecy," but criticizes them for being inconsistent in other areas.[464]

Louis Berkhof critiques premillennialism as a theory "based on a literal interpretation of the prophetic delineations of the future of Israel and of the Kingdom of God, which is entirely untenable."[465] He adds, "The New Testament certainly does not favor the literalism of the

---

[462] S. Lewis Johnson, "Paul and "the Israel of God" an Exegetical and Eschatological Case Study, in *The Master's Seminary Journal*, 20/1 (Spring, 2009): 54.
[463] Oswald T. Allis, *Prophecy and the Church* (Phillipsburg, NJ: Presbyterian and Reformed, 1945), 16.
[464] Allis, 21.
[465] Louis Berkhof, *Systematic Theology* (Grand Rapids, MI: Eerdmans, 1974), 712.

Premillenarians. Moreover, this literalism lands them in all kinds of absurdities..."⁴⁶⁶

John Gerstner takes an important step in recognizing that the distinctions aren't simply hermeneutic, but also theological – specifically regarding pre-commitment to theological conclusions:

> We all agree that most literature, including the Bible, is usually meant to be understood according to the literal construction of the words which are used....At the point where we differ, there is a tendency for the dispensationalists to be literalistic where the non-dispensationalist tends to interpret the Bible figuratively. But to say on the basis of that limited divergence of interpretation that the two schools represent fundamentally different approaches is not warranted. Many on both sides think that this minor "hermeneutical" difference is a more foundational difference than the theological. We profoundly disagree for we believe that the dispensational literal hermeneutic is driven by an *a priori* commitment to dispensational theological distinctives."⁴⁶⁷

While I believe Gerstner understates the hermeneutical disagreement and accuses the wrong side of theological pre-commitment, he is right to emphasize the importance of theological pre-commitment, since such *presuppositions*

---

⁴⁶⁶ Berkhof, 713.
⁴⁶⁷ John Gerstner, *Wrongly Dividing the Word of Truth* (Morgan, PA: Soli Deo Gloria, 2000), 92-93.

are a part of theological method and can have a tremendous impact on hermeneutical principles.

Robert Saucy makes a slightly different argument than the aforementioned TR thinkers. He suggests that,

> An analysis of non-dispensational systems, however, reveals that their less-than literal approach to Israel in the Old Testament prophecies does not really arise from an a priori spiritualistic or metaphorical hermeneutic. Rather it is the result of their interpretation of the New Testament using the same grammatico-historical hermeneutic as that of dispensationalists...So the fundamental issue between dispensationalists and non-dispensationalists is neither a basic hermeneutic principle nor the ultimate purpose of human history. The basic issue is the way we understand the historical plan and the goal of that plan through which God will bring eternal glory to himself.[468]

While Saucy downplays hermeneutic distinctions even more than does Gerstner, Saucy still recognizes the differences exist, but attributes them to a broader, rather than narrower, theological understanding. Hence, while there are differences regarding the extent of the hermeneutic differences and the exact nature of the theological disagreement, there seems to be a common recognition that the differences between dispensational

---

[468] Robert Saucy, *The Case for Progressive Dispensationalism* (Grand Rapids, MI: Zondervan, 1993), 20.

Epilogue: The Importance of How We Interpret the Bible 173

and TR thought are (1) primarily theological and hermeneutic, and (2) found largely in prophetic passages.

Premise 3: Dispensationalism has historically agreed with fundamental aspects of TR soteriology, while disagreeing on some points (as illustrated by Chafer).

Lewis Sperry Chafer accomplished inestimable gains for dispensational soteriology and sanctification, as his *Systematic Theology* remains to this day arguably the most comprehensive dispensational work on both topics. While Chafer's volumes are tremendously helpful, they also betray an important reliance on TR thought, as evidenced by Chafer's own theological method. Chafer suggests that "theology may be extended properly to include all material and immaterial realities that exist and the facts concerning them and contained in them."[469] This curiously broad characterization is advanced in his definition of systematic theology, which he describes as, "A science which follows a humanly devised scheme or order of doctrinal development and which purports to incorporate into its system all the truth about God and His universe *from any and every source* [emphasis mine].[470] Chafer admits that his source material for the systematic theology is much broader than the Scriptures themselves (though he acknowledges that Biblical theology relies exclusively on Scripture).

A further methodological characteristic of Chafer's theology is his proclivity to include large portions of quoted material – not to illustrate ideas, but to state

---

[469] LS Chafer, *Systematic Theology, Vol. 1* (Grand Rapids, MI: Kregel, 1993), 3.
[470] Chafer, *Vol. 1*, 5.

them initially, as primary source material. This approach is not unique to Chafer, being characteristic of his times. However, this penchant for relying on secondary source data as primary, and his methodological admission that secondary source material may have equal standing with Scripture is troubling for the development of dispensational theology.

To illustrate the influence of these two methodological traits on Chafer's theology, note his first extended quote of the volume on soteriology. The initial quotation includes no less than three full pages reproduced from W. Lindsay Alexander's *System of Biblical Theology*, on the accomplishment of Jesus's death. Chafer introduces the quote by saying that Alexander "discusses this feature of Soteriology in a manner well suited to this thesis."[471] Chafer offers a remark immediately following the quote: "In conclusion it may be observed…"[472] Instead of building his theology directly and exclusively from Scripture, Chafer imports a tremendous portion of the doctrine of atonement from Alexander's work. That is not to say that Alexander is either right or wrong, only to acknowledge that he was steeped in TR thinking,[473] and Chafer allowed him to have a significant role in the newly systematized dispensational understanding of the atonement.

---

[471] LS Chafer, *Systematic Theology, Vol. 3* (Grand Rapids, MI: Kregel, 1993), 68.
[472] Chafer, *Vol. 3*, 72.
[473] E.g., Alexander's supersessionism is evident in James Ross, *W. Lindsay Alexander, D.D., L.L.D.,: His Life and Work* (London: James Nisbet & Co., 1887), 267 and 330.

Epilogue: The Importance of How We Interpret the Bible 175

To his credit, in the spirit of scholastic integrity, Chafer also extensively quoted those with whom he disagreed. In the same volume, Chafer allows John Miley a six-page quotation, but only so out of respect for Miley's scholarship on the issue of the governmental theory of the atonement.[474] Chafer concludes his chapter on the atonement with a *ten-page* quotation of B.B. Warfield's "Modern Theories of the Atonement," lauding Warfield's address as "the most clarifying analysis of this subject ever published.[475]

By contrast, Chafer's volume on eschatology shows a reluctance to rely on TR sources. Besides the introduction (in which he quotes numerous TR thinkers to illustrate the importance of eschatology) and the section discussing the history of chiliasm (where one expects and finds a number of quotes from historical sources), with two exceptions Chafer only quotes extensively from C.I Scofield,[476] Frederick Taylor,[477] H.A. Ironside,[478] Henry Thiessen,[479] Ford Ottman,[480] and J.J. Van Oosterzee,[481] all dispensational thinkers in their eschatology. As for the exceptions, Chafer cites George Peters, but only to agree with Peters' argument that we should pay more attention to the Davidic Covenant,[482] and he cites B.B. Warfield,

---

[474] Chafer, *Vol. 3*, 147-152.
[475] Chafer, *Vol. 3*, 155ff.
[476] LS Chafer, *Systematic Theology, Vol. 4* (Grand Rapids, MI: Kregel, 1993), 286-287; 311-312; 357-358; 413-414.
[477] Chafer, *Vol. 4*, 307-311.
[478] Chafer, *Vol. 4*, 335-336.
[479] Chafer, *Vol. 4*, 338; 348-349; 361-363; 369-370.
[480] Chafer, *Vol. 4*, 354-357.
[481] Chafer, *Vol. 4*, 423-426.
[482] Chafer, *Vol. 4*, 324-325.

but only to compare historical views on immortality in the eternal state.[483]

My point here is not to impeach Chafer or his scholarship, but simply to demonstrate that his theology – the most comprehensive theology dispensationalism has yet produced – allows TR thought to do some heavy lifting in certain key areas, while restricting TR influence in others – and that by Chafer's own design. Later influential thinkers would capitalize on this, attempting to bring definition to areas that remained otherwise underdeveloped in Chafer's dispensational thought, but doing so in deference especially to TR thought.

Premise 4: An explanation for the soteriological similarities is found centrally in the shared methodology of appealing to TR authorities (as illustrated by MacArthur and Piper).

Self-identified *leaky dispensationalist*, John MacArthur pursued clarification in the areas of soteriology and sanctification by blasting Chaferian thinking for not being consistent enough with reformed thought (my words, not his). MacArthur critiques Thomas Constable's view that "not everyone who believes the gospel realizes that the Savior has the right to be sovereign over his life."[484] MacArthur asserts, "Along with everyone else who rejects the Savior's right to be sovereign, that person is an unbeliever..."[485] It seems

---

[483] Chafer, *Vol. 4*, 421.
[484] Thomas Constable, "The Gospel Message" in *Walvoord: A Tribute* (Chicago, IL: Moody Press, 1982), 203.
[485] John MacArthur, *The Gospel According to Jesus* (Grand Rapids, MI: Zondervan, 1994), 75.

Epilogue: The Importance of How We Interpret the Bible

obvious that MacArthur's critique misrepresents what Constable said (Constable did not suggest that one could reject His lordship and be saved, but only that one could not fully comprehend it and still be saved). MacArthur later pans Constable's statement that "Repentance means to change one's mind; it does not mean to change one's life."[486] MacArthur cites Charles Ryrie and Michael Cocoris as being erroneous on this same issue.[487] Instead, MacArthur prefers J.I. Packer's, Louis Berkhof's, and Geerhardus Vos's definitions of repentance, quoting sympathetically all three.[488]

MacArthur understands that Chafer's soteriology departs from TR thinking in some areas. MacArthur cites, for example, "Chafer's dichotomy between carnal and spiritual Christians" as a teaching previously shown erroneous by B.B. Warfield.[489] Notably, MacArthur attributes his own departure from dispensational thinking on that point as *methodological*, as he observes this issue to be "a classic example of how dispensationalism's methodology can be carried too far."[490] MacArthur, favoring the understandings of A.W. Tozer and James Boice over Charles Ryrie and Michael Cocoris.[491] synthesizes salvation and discipleship, perceiving them not as two steps, but as a single process. He says,

---

[486] MacArthur, 177.
[487] MacArthur, 177.
[488] MacArthur, 179.
[489] MacArthur, 30-31.
[490] MacArthur, 31.
[491] MacArthur, 34-37.

> Those who teach that obedience and submission are extraneous to saving faith are forced to make a firm but unbiblical distinction between salvation and discipleship. This dichotomy, like that of the carnal/spiritual Christian, sets up two classes of Christians: believers only and true disciples.[492]

In soteriological areas, MacArthur exhibits a preference for TR doctrine and tradition. Note, for example, the similarity between how John MacArthur and John Piper handle the issue of limited atonement. MacArthur holds to Calvinism's five points, including limited atonement (the "l" in TULIP). He departs from his generally literal hermeneutic in handling 1 John 2:2, arguing that ὅλου τοῦ κόσμου does not refer to the whole world. He adds, "Jesus didn't pay for the sins of Judas...or Adolf Hitler."[493] MacArthur explains that the verse is simply explaining that atonement was now available to the whole world, but that it does not mean that Jesus paid for the sins of the whole world. Appealing to John 11:52, MacArthur asserts Jesus only died on behalf of the children of God. But 11:51 describes that Jesus would die for the nation [of Israel.] Still, 11:51-52 makes no claim that Jesus would die for the children of God, but only that He died in order to gather them together. MacArthur's presupposed limited atonement drives his (non) exegesis of 1 John 2:2. When John says

---

[492] MacArthur, 36.
[493] John MacArthur "John MacArthur – Limited Atonement: Explained – 1 John 2:2" (YouTube video) at http://www.youtube.com/watch?v=DepxyWF8euA.

Epilogue: The Importance of How We Interpret the Bible

"the whole world" he really means "the whole world...*except for anyone in the whole world who would not believe in Him.*"

John Piper agrees with MacArthur, and defends his own conclusion almost identically: "When Christ died on the cross paying the price for us...He decisively accomplished that for His own. His sheep. His elect...He didn't just make it accomplishable, He accomplished it."[494] In other words, when Jesus declared that it was finished, He had completed the entire redemptive process for believers. For this reason, Piper prefers the term "triumphantly effective atonement" instead of limited atonement. Referring to John 3:16, Piper admits that "the cross is universal in that conditional sense," that anyone believing will have life.

Jesus "decisively purchased with a dowry, His bride," Piper says. In handling 1 John 2:2, Piper identifies Jesus as the "wrath remover" for the whole world, and like MacArthur, likens the passage to John 11:51-52 – a passage which again, *does not limit His death to the children of God.* Piper adds, "I think that is what he means by propitiation for the whole world, namely, as the gospel spreads around the whole world, the whole world becomes the object of His saving work in that He gathers children of God from out of every tribe and tongue." But John didn't say in 1 John 2:2 that Jesus died for people *from* the whole world, but that He was the ἱλασμός, the propitiation περὶ ὅλου τοῦ κόσμου – for or *on behalf of* the whole world.

---

[494] John Piper, "John Piper on Limited Atonement" (YouTube video) at http://www.youtube.com/watch?v=tZEIPPgMkFA.

Both Piper and MacArthur are playing a semantic game here, and neither can deal with the exact phrasing of 1 John 2:2. Both refer to a distant context that is dissimilar in wording, and both redefine *the whole world* to mean *not the whole world*. The very simple problem they are trying to avoid – that Jesus's propitiation must be a completed purchase, and thus must be fully efficacious – is a theological/philosophical problem, not an exegetical one. They are trying to resolve a philosophical conundrum that isn't there by explaining away the passage that is there. In fact, there is no problem at all – they are assuming too much of the word ἱλασμός, without any exegetical warrant to do so. Romans 3:25-26 distinguishes between propitiation (ἱλαστήριον) and justification (δικαιοῦντα). There is no exegetical need to conclude that justification of the elect occurred at the cross. It didn't. The justification is through faith, and has always been (Gen 15: 6; Rom 3:26).

Also, this argument favoring limited atonement takes the sheep/shepherd metaphor too far. Shepherds don't create their sheep (Jn 1), nor do shepherds hold their sheep together in every way (Col 1), nor are shepherds priests on behalf of their sheep (Heb 4), nor do shepherds choose their sheep before the foundation of the world (Eph 1). The metaphor in John 10 simply serves to illustrate how the sheep enter the fold (10:1-6) – through the shepherd. The figure of speech doesn't go much further than that. A sheep is one who enters through the shepherd (10:2), and His disbelieving audiences were not sheep because they didn't come to the Father through Him (10:26). In other words, He puts it on their shoulders that they are not sheep — it is their fault. Jesus is not referring to election here at all.

The formal quality of this limited atonement assertion is not problematic, but the truth-value is. Piper's and MacArthur's appeals to John 10:11 (sheep) or 11:52 (children of God) is a valid (in form) modus ponens argument:

> P1: If Jesus died for the sheep (or the children of God) then He didn't die for those who weren't sheep (or the children of God).
> P2: Jesus died for the sheep (or the children of God).
> C: Jesus didn't die for those who weren't sheep (or the children of God).

In a deductive argument, if the two premises are true, then the conclusion will necessarily follow. The problem is simply that P1 is not exegetically defensible (there is no passage which supports such a thing, and 1 John 2:2 seems to strongly assert the opposite view). If there is no exegetical evidence for the assertion, then it is *not demonstrably true*. In order to solve a nonexistent problem, these two intelligent men appeal to *an exegetical assumption and state it as fact*. MacArthur and Piper are able to find tight agreement in these conclusions because they are employing common methodology.

Premise 5: TR methodology is compatible with an open but cautious view on non-cessationism.

Chafer says little about the closure of the canon in his Systematic Theology, making only brief observations in his volume on bibliology, but what he does say is dispensationally significant:

> The formal closing of the New Testament canon is at least intimated in Revelation 22:18. The dissimilarity in the manner in which the two Testaments end is significant. All the unfulfilled expectation of the Old Testament is articulate as that Testament closes and the last verses give assurance of the coming of another prophet. But no continued revelation is impending as the New Testament is terminated; rather that announcement is made that the Lord Himself will soon return and the natural conclusion is that there would be no further voice speaking from heaven before the trumpet heralds the second advent of Christ.[495]

Rather than relying on a single passage (or on any appeal to a previous theological tradition) to make his case here, Chafer's assertion that the canon is closed rests commendably upon the whole of progressive revelation considered synthetically and chronologically. Chafer's appeal to a synthetic view of Scripture is characteristic of classical dispensational thought, as illustrated by

---

[495] LS Chafer, *Systematic Theology, Vol. 1* (Grand Rapids, MI: Kregel, 1993), 93.

Scofield's emphasis on Biblical synthesis.[496] This synthetic approach, simple though it is, underscores a commitment to the Biblical narrative on its own terms, and literally understood.

Chafer gives but a little attention to 1 Corinthians 13:8, suggesting that, "it is possible that the averment that prophecy shall 'cease' (1 Cor. 13:8) anticipates the close of the New Testament canon; for where there is no divinely designated and duly attested prophet there is no Scripture to be received or delivered."[497] In a later discussion on the nature of spiritual gifts, Chafer quotes John Walvoord extensively, including Walvoord's acknowledgement that by individual exposition of each gift, it is evident that there are "gifts known by the early Christians, which seem to have passed from the scene with the apostolic period. Some of these are claimed for today by certain sects, whose neglect of the Scriptural instructions for use of these gifts is in itself a testimony to the spurious quality of their affected gifts."[498] Walvoord's comment marks dispensationalism's attention to both synthesis and exegesis in considering spiritual gifts. For good measure, Charles Ryrie discusses the canon in historical and theological terms, to illustrate that a

---

[496] See C.I. Scofield, *Scofield Bible Correspondence Course Volume I: Introduction to the Scriptures* (Chicago, IL: Moody Press, 1959), 12.
[497] Chafer, *Vol. 1*, 101.
[498] LS Chafer, *Systematic Theology, Vol. 6* (Grand Rapids, MI: Kregel, 1993), 220.

dispensational perspective on the canon is consistent with dominant historic perspectives of the early church.[499]

The testimony of the later church is mixed. For example, John Chrysostom referred to the gifts' "cessation, being such as then used to occur but now no longer take place.[500] Augustine initially described tongues as "done for a betokening, and it passed away,"[501] and early on he held to a cessationist position:

> When the Catholic Church had been founded and diffused throughout the whole world, on the one hand miracles were not allowed to continue till our time, lest the mind should always seek visible things, and the human race should grow cold by becoming accustomed to things which when they were novelties kindled its faith…[502]

Despite Augustine's early sentiments, his personal experiences over the years caused him to take another position:

> It is sometimes objected that the miracles, which Christians claim to have occurred, no longer

---

[499] Charles Ryrie, *Basic Theology* (Wheaton, IL: Victor Books, 1986), 105-109
[500] John Chrysostom, *Homilies on the Epistles of Paul to the Corinthians* (Grand Rapids, MI: CCEL), XXIX: 169.
[501] Augustine, *Homilies on the First Epistle of John,* trans. H. Browne, ed. P. Schaff, 6:10, at http://www.newadvent.org/fathers/1702.htm.
[502] *Of True Religion* 47, from J.H.S. Burleigh, (ed.), *Augustine: Earlier Writings, Library of Christian Classics,* (Philadelphia, PA: Westminster Press, 1953), 6, 248.

happen...The truth is that even today miracles are being wrought in the name of Christ."⁵⁰³

Even while defending the existence of miraculous signs, Augustine maintained that the canon was indeed closed.⁵⁰⁴ Still, Augustine introduced an experiential element to his often otherwise rationalistic approach. That experiential component would play a substantial role in the later TR sympathy to the non-cessationist viewpoint.

Aquinas adds important commentary to the cessationist debate. He describes miracles in the present tense as serving two purposes: "in one way for the confirmation of truth declared, in another way in proof of a person's holiness."⁵⁰⁵ While charismatic gifts are possible, they are not common, as he quotes Augustine to say, "the reason these are not granted to all holy men is lets by a most baneful error the weak be deceived into thinking such deeds to imply greater gifts than the outwards signs of righteousness."⁵⁰⁶ One can see the fruit of Aquinas's thinking in the Catholic doctrine of sainthood, which requires that the candidate for sainthood demonstrate "heroic virtue."⁵⁰⁷

---

⁵⁰³ Augustine, *The City of God*, abridged from trans. Walsh, Zema, Monahan, Honan (New York, NY: Image Books, 1958), 22:8, 512-513
⁵⁰⁴ Augustine, 22:8.
⁵⁰⁵ Thomas Aquinas, *Summa Theologica* (Grand Rapids, Mi: CCEL), II, Q. 178.
⁵⁰⁶ Aquinas, *Summa*, II, Q. 178.
⁵⁰⁷ *Catholic Catechism*, 828.

While Aquinas was open to charismatic gifts in some instances, he adds that 1 Corinthians 13 "is not speaking here about the cessation of spiritual gifts through mortal sin, but rather about the cessation of spiritual gifts which pertain to this life through supervening glory."[508] Regarding the cessation of prophecy he says, "in future glory prophecy will have no place..."[509] Of tongues, he observes, "some in the early Church spoke in various tongues...in future glory each one will understand each tongue. Hence, it will not be necessary to speak in various tongues."[510] Aquinas is a cessationist only in the sense that he recognizes that the charismatic gifts will be unnecessary in future glory, and in that he acknowledges they were utilized in the early church particularly, but his open approach looks very much like the open-but-cautious view of today.

The Reformers espoused a cessationist view, in part to counter Catholic claims of miracles as confirmation of unorthodox doctrines. To their credit, the Reformers, in accordance with sola scriptura, sought to ground their arguments exegetically. Luther is resolute in his cessationist stance, asserting that "Once the Church had been established and properly advertised by these miracles, the visible appearance of the Holy Ghost ceased."[511] Calvin's perspective on healing is similar: "But

---

[508] Thomas Aquinas, *Commentary on the First Epistle to the Corinthians*, trans. Fabian Lercher, electronic edition at http://dhspriory.org/thomas/SS1Cor.htm, 787.
[509] Aquinas, *First Corinthians*, 788.
[510] Aquinas, *First Corinthians*, 789.
[511] Martin Luther, *Commentary on St. Paul's Epistle to the Galatians* (Grand Rapids, MI: CCEL, 1991), 84.

that gift of healing, like the rest of the miracles, which the Lord willed to be brought forth for a time, has vanished away in order to make the new preaching of the gospel marvelous forever."[512] Jon Mark Ruthven identifies key components of Calvin's cessationism in particular: miracles were for the confirming of Scripture, not post-scriptural teaching, and Catholic miracles were consequently self-evidently false.[513] Further, while Calvin held to cessationism, he left a window open to the possibility that such gifts could potentially have a present or future use in the church.[514] Ruthven observes another important component in Calvin's thought: namely that Calvin borrows Aquinas's approach to associating the charismata with the accreditation of Scripture without attempting systematically to prove the connection.[515] This is significant because it shows that the Reformers in some instances borrowed from thomistic traditions without earning the doctrines for themselves. Modern TR methodology is not unique in its tradition of appealing to theological authorities.

Whereas Aquinas and the Reformers held to varying degrees of cessationism and openness, B.B. Warfield's cessationism was unmistakably closed. He argued that miracles were,

---

[512] John Calvin, *Institutes of the Christian Religion*, trans. Ford Battles (Philadelphia, PA: Westminster Press, 1940), 4:19:18.
[513] Jon Mark Ruthven, *On the Cessation of the Charismata: The Protestant Polemic on Post-Biblical Miracles* (Sheffield, UK: University of Sheffield Academic Press, 2009), 22.
[514] See Ruthven, footnote 22 on page 22.
[515] Ruthven, 23.

> The characterizing peculiarity of specifically the Apostolic Church, and it belonged therefore exclusively to the Apostoloic age...These gifts were not possession of the primitive Christian as such; nor for that matter of the Apostolic Church or the Apostolic age for themselves; they were distinctively the authentication of the Apostles...This does not mean, of course, that only the Apostles appear in the New Testament as working miracles, or that they alone are represented as recipients of the charismata. But it does mean that the charismata belonged, in a true sense, to the Apostles, and constituted one of the true signs of an Apostle.[516]

Warfield appeals primarily (in the early context of his argument) to theologians of the post-Reformation era who he says "taught with great distinctness that the charismata ceased with the Apostolic age."[517] He offers roughly fifteen pages of historical and theological data before introducing his first Biblical citation (a mention of Acts 8:14-17),[518] and that lone reference is the only Biblical citation in the entire opening chapter that discusses his cessationism. In fact, the only references to Scripture in the remaining two hundred pages are Mark 16:17-18,[519] Matthew 8:17,[520] James 5:14-16,[521] John

---

[516] B.B. Warfield, *Counterfeit Miracles* (New York, NY: Scribner and Sons, 1918), 6 and 21.
[517] Warfield, 6.
[518] Warfield, 22.
[519] Warfield, 48, 166-169.
[520] Warfield, 166, 174-177.

14:12-13,[522] and 1 Corinthians 12,[523] and these are considered only in the context of an apologetic specifically contra the teachings of A.J. Gordon. Once again, as we have seen before with Thomas and the Reformers, the method for deriving doctrinal conclusions is more related to historical rather than Biblical theology. Whether or not Warfield's conclusions are correct is not the central issue. Warfield's work is respected as the most influential cessationist apologetic to that point,[524] yet, by the design of its author, the work attempts almost no attention to exegetical or synthetic grounding.

More recently, John MacArthur has been a leading advocate for cessationism. MacArthur's *Charismatic Chaos* attempts a Biblical response to the charismatic movement, and succeeds more than most. Like Chafer, MacArthur begins his defense of a closed canon by appealing to a synthetic view of Scripture:

> When the canon closed on the Old Testament after the time of Ezra and Nehemiah, there followed four hundred "silent years" when no prophet spoke God's revelation in any form. That silence was broken by John the Baptist as God spoke once more prior to the New Testament age. God then moved various men to record the books of the New Testament, and the last of these was Revelation....Just as the close of the Old

---

[521] Warfield, 166, 169-173, 187.
[522] Warfield, 167, 173-174.
[523] Warfield, 167, 173.
[524] Ruthven, 29.

Testament canon was followed by silence, so the close of the New Testament has been followed by the utter absence of new revelation in any form.[525]

Initially, MacArthur correctly appeals to a synthetic perspective, however, unlike Chafer, he then immediately turns to the TR method of appealing to historical authority when he adds, "Since the book of Revelation was completed, no new written or verbal prophecy has ever been universally recognized by Christians as divine truth from God."[526] The first part of his argument is textual (and objectively verifiable), but the *evidence* of his argument is historical and subjective. This is a specific example of how mixed methods can weaken a case. MacArthur demonstrates further admixture of the objective and subjective in order to justify his cessationism.

Introducing the topic of the cessation of tongues, MacArthur proclaims, "I am convinced by history, theology, and the Bible that tongues ceased in the apostolic age."[527] Note the order of the evidence: history and theology (two subjective disciplines) come before the Bible (objective truth). *Why?* This order of priority seems a common characteristic of TR methodology. He adds, "Tongues were therefore a sign of transition between the Old and New Covenants. With the establishment of the church, a new day had dawned for the people of

---

[525] John MacArthur, *Charismatic Chaos* (Grand Rapids, MI: Zondervan, 1992), 71-72.
[526] MacArthur, *Charismatic Chaos*, 72.
[527] MacArthur, *Charismatic Chaos*, 281.

God...once the period of transition was past, the sign was no longer necessary."[528] Notice the vague appeal to at least some degree of supersessionism (if tongues is no longer in play, then according to MacArthur's assertion, the New Covenant is presently being fulfilled). To that end, MacArthur quotes reformed scholar O. Palmer Robertson to confirm that, "the transition [between Old and New Covenants] has been made."[529] MacArthur not only finds himself on slippery methodological footing, but by this maneuver he has connected his cessationism with the *full blown supersessionism* that Robertson advocates!

Further, MacArthur asks the question, "What evidence is there that tongues have ceased?"[530] His answer is first theological, and then historical: "History records that tongues did cease."[531] He adds based on the historical and theological evidence, "Thus we conclude that from the end of the apostolic era to the beginning of the twentieth century there were no genuine occurrences of the New Testament gift of tongues."[532] In all this, he has not offered an *exegetical basis* for the cessation of tongues. Once again, the issue is not whether the conclusions are correct, but whether the manner in which the conclusions are derived are legitimate. Consequently, he has left the door open for historical and theological reinterpretations that would call into question his cessationist conclusion.

---

[528] MacArthur, *Charismatic Chaos*, 282-283.
[529] MacArthur, *Charismatic Chaos*, 283.
[530] MacArthur, *Charismatic Chaos*, 282.
[531] MacArthur, *Charismatic Chaos*, 283.
[532] MacArthur, *Charismatic Chaos*, 286.

John Piper provides just such a reinterpretation. In a sermon on spiritual gifts, Piper notes, "I think it would be fair to say also from this text that you shouldn't bend your mind too much trying to label your spiritual gift before you use it. That is, don't worry about whether you can point to prophecy, or teaching, or wisdom, or knowledge, or healing, or miracles, or mercy, or administration, etc..."[533] His open-but-casual approach comes across as relevant and non-dogmatic (I think this approach is a major factor in his broad appeal). On March 5 [1984], Piper discussed a survey to determine Bethlehem's "Charismatic Quotient," and expressed that "Truth is not determined by counting noses...Let's study the word together and see if our 'Charismatic Quotient' is too high or too low."[534] Notice how he has apparently shifted from historic TR methodology to take a more exegetical posture. In the discussion, Piper proposes four theses on the NT gift of prophecy:

1. It is still valid and useful for the church today. He asserts that this is the clear implication of 1 Corinthians 13:8-12 and Acts 2:17-18.
2. It is a Spirit-prompted, Spirit-sustained, utterance that is rooted in a true revelation (1 Corinthians 14:30), but is fallible because the prophet's perception of the revelation, and

---

[533] John Piper, *Spiritual Gifts* (sermon), March 15, 1981, at http://www.desiringgod.org/resource-library/sermons/spiritual-gifts.

[534] John Piper, Testing Bethlehem's Charismatic Quotient (sermon), March 4, 1984, at http://www.desiringgod.org/resource-library/taste-see-articles/testing-bethlehems-charismatic-quotient.

Epilogue: The Importance of How We Interpret the Bible 193

   thinking about the revelation, and report of the revelation are all fallible. It is thus similar to the gift of teaching which is Spirit-prompted, Spirit sustained, rooted in an infallible revelation (the Bible), and yet is fallible but very useful to the church.
3. It does not have an authority that is on a par with Scripture, for Scripture is verbally inspired, not just Spirit-prompted and Spirit-sustained. The very words of the biblical writers are the words of God (1 Corinthians 2:13; 2 Timothy 3:16). This is not true of the words that come from the "gift of prophecy."
4. The New Testament gift of prophecy is a "third category" of prophetic utterance between the categories of 1) verbally inspired, intrinsically authoritative, infallible speech spoken by the likes of Moses, Jesus and the apostles; and 2) the speech of false prophets spoken presumptuously, without inspiration and liable to condemnation (Deuteronomy 18:20). Those two categories (absolutely infallible vs. false) do not exhaust all the biblical teaching on prophecy.[535]

The *study of the word* that Piper offered turned out to be almost entirely theological rather than exegetical – none of the theses Piper proposed are exegetically defensible

---

[535] John Piper, The New Testament Gift of Prophecy (sermon), March 26, 1990, at http://www.desiringgod.org/resource-library/taste-see-articles/the-new-testament-gift-of-prophecy.

from the passages he cites, and he doesn't even attempt such a defense. Granted, the context is sermonic, but much of what Piper writes is equally homiletic. Evidently, Piper does not depart from TR methodology. Instead, he re-labels it with an attractive and casual *study the word* tag.

As Piper discusses signs and wonders, he declares, "I am one of those Baptist General Conference people who believes that 'signs and wonders' and all the spiritual gifts of 1 Corinthians 12:8-10 are valid for today and should be 'earnestly desired' (1 Corinthians 14:1) for the edification of the church and the spread of the gospel... if signs and wonders were not limited in function to validating the ministry of Jesus and the apostles, but rather had a role in the edifying and evangelistic work of the church in general, then there is good reason to trust God for their proper use today."[536] Good reason, based on what? Piper's interpretation of 1 Corinthians 13:8-12 is the definitive factor in his advocating of signs and wonders for the present day church. Piper's entire argument is worthy of reproducing here:

> So the answer to the question of when the perfect comes and when the imperfect gifts pass away is the "then" of verse 12, namely, the time of seeing "face to face" and "understanding as we are understood." When will this happen? Both of these phrases ("seeing face to face" and "understanding

---

[536] John Piper, Signs and Wonders: Then and Now (sermon), February 1, 1991, at http://www.desiringgod.org/resource-library/articles/signs-and-wonders-then-and-now.

as we have been understood") are stretched beyond the breaking point if we say that they refer to the closing of the New Testament canon or the close of the apostolic age. Rather, they refer to our experience at the second coming of Jesus. Then "we shall see him as he is" (1 John 3:2) The phrase "face to face" in the Greek Old Testament refers to seeing God personally (Genesis 32:30; Judges 6:22). Thomas Edwards' hundred-year-old commentary is right to say, "When the perfect is come at the advent of Christ, then the Christian will know God intuitively and directly, even as he was before known of God" (First Epistle to the Corinthians, p. 353, italics added).

This means that verse 10 can be paraphrased, "When Christ returns, the imperfect will pass away." And since "the imperfect" refers to spiritual gifts like prophecy and knowledge and tongues, we may paraphrase further, "When Christ returns, then prophecy and knowledge and tongues will pass away."

Here is a definite statement about the time of the cessation of spiritual gifts, and that time is the second coming of Christ. Richard Gaffin does not do justice to the actual wording of verse 10 when he says, "The time of the cessation of prophecy and tongues is an open question so far as this passage is concerned" (Perspectives on Pentecost, p. 111). It is not an open question. Paul says, "When the perfect comes [at that time, not

> before or after], the imperfect [gifts like prophecy and tongues, etc.] will pass away."
>
> Therefore, 1 Corinthians 13:8-12 teaches that such spiritual gifts will continue until the second coming of Jesus. There is no reason to exclude from this conclusion the other "imperfect" gifts mentioned in 1 Corinthians 12:8-10. Since these include miracles, faith, healings, etc., with which we associate "signs and wonders", there is clear New Testament warrant for expecting that "signs and wonders" will continue until Jesus comes.[537]

Notice Piper's two-pronged appeal to historical authorities (Thomas Edwards' "hundred year old commentary"), and to English context-connecting without anything but anecdotal exegetical attention to the original languages (1 Jn 3:2 [ὅτι ὀψόμεθα αὐτὸν καθώς ἐστιν] and 1 Cor 13:12 [τότε δὲ πρόσωπον πρὸς πρόσωπον] are not at all similar in the Greek).

By formalizing Piper's argument, we can see that his method for handling 1 Corinthians 13:8-12 is an attempt at logic-based rather than exegetical articulation. Further, his argument is neither sound nor are the premises accurate. His argument demonstrates a core interpretive problem in the spiritual gifts debate:

> P1: Both phrases ("seeing face to face" and "understanding as we have been understood") are

---

[537] Ibid.

stretched beyond the breaking point if we say that they refer to the closing of the New Testament canon or the close of the apostolic age. [Based on what textual authority?]

P2: Then "we shall see him as he is" (1 John 3:2) The phrase "face to face" in the Greek Old Testament refers to seeing God personally (Genesis 32:30; Judges 6:22). [Invoking a dissimilar distant context contributes nothing to the exegesis of 1 Cor 13:12]

P3: Thomas Edwards' hundred-year-old commentary is right to say, "When the perfect is come at the advent of Christ, then the Christian will know God intuitively and directly, even as he was before known of God" (First Epistle to the Corinthians, p. 353, italics added). [This offers nothing objective for understanding the definition of τὸ τέλειον then. The age of Edwards or his commentary is irrelevant.]

Conclusion: Therefore, 1 Corinthians 13:8-12 teaches that such spiritual gifts will continue until the second coming of Jesus.

The argument includes a series of subjective assertions and a conclusion unsupported by the premises, and hence is nothing more than a non sequitur. Yet this is the argument offered to answer the central question of when the revelatory gifts of 1 Corinthians 13 will conclude.

Piper's open-but-casual conclusion represents a dominant strand in evangelical theology. It is clear we have lost our methodological way.

Mark Driscoll, representing an emergent/reformed version of TR methodology, characterizes cessationism as "a clever way of saying we don't need [the Holy Spirit] like we used to...that's not true."[538] While Driscoll is guilty here of false dichotomy, he criticizes cessationists for employing that very logical fallacy:

> And so their argument even comes down to 1st Corinthians 13 which gets turned into origami, right? When the perfect comes the imperfect disappears, we'll see him face to face, the perfect is Jesus. The perfect is Jesus. But then what happens is, to defend this sort of modernistic rationalistic, cessationistic position, we throw up the craziest kooks in the charismatic camp and say well you don't want that do ya? uh no, no we don't. If it's nothing or that it's a real coin flip, cause neither is the real win.[539]

Driscoll's false dichotomy, though not as elegant as Piper's suggestive non sequitur, is not dissimilar to Piper's brand of non-cessationism, and is probably equally as influential.

---

[538] Mark Driscoll "Don't Elevate Doctrine above the Holy Spirit" (YouTube video) at
http://www.youtube.com/watch?v=XUXfHaHUkvo.
[539] Frank Turk "Open Letter to Mark Driscoll" at
http://teampyro.blogspot.com/2011/08/open-letter-to-mark-driscoll.html.

Piper and Driscoll are only two among a host of contemporary examples illustrating the compatibility of TR methodology and open views on non-cessation. Piper and Driscoll also exemplify how present-day applications of TR methodology seem, in fact, to prefer non-cessationism, as these applications offer no means for objective grounding of cessationism.

Conclusion: As long as dispensationalism appeals to TR methodology for any of its doctrines, inconsistencies identifiable in TR eschatology and soterology will be present within dispensational thought. With respect to the cessationism debate, this means dispensationalism will have increasing difficulty in arguing against non-cessationism unless it abandons TR methodology altogether.

The example afforded by MacArthur's soteriological and ecclesiological compatibility with TR thinking and incompatibility with Chaferian thinking underscores three key points. First, Chafer defends his views on the atonement with heavy reliance on TR thought, so when MacArthur defends his lordship, limited atonement, and cessationist views with appeals to the same authority as does Chafer, there appears little methodological difference between the two camps. Chafer builds large portions of his soteriology with TR materials, but where Chafer departs from TR thinking, MacArthur reproves Chafer with nothing more than TR ideas. The point here is that Chafer illustrates dispensationalism's reticence to apply the same method to soteriology and ecclesiology as to eschatology, and the result is theological inconsistency.

Second, these divergences in soteriology and ecclesiology betray a splintering in dispensational thinking. MacArthur's brand of TR soteriology and ecclesiology is a dominant strand in dispensational thought, in large part due to its historic appeal to widely appreciated TR thinking. MacArthur illustrates well the division, as he coolly rejects dispensational ideas that disagree with TR thinking, but only up to the point where there remains a distinction between Israel and the church. For some reason (indiscernible to me, since MacArthur is not grounded in a consistently literal hermeneutic), that is where MacArthur and his many followers draw the line. As lordship salvation becomes increasingly popular among younger evangelicals in general (see, New Calvinism, and the Young, Restless, Reformed), dispensationalists seem both increasingly sympathetic to lordship salvation and limited atonement, and increasingly unwilling to challenge the TR methodology that fosters these trends. Consequently, it comes as no surprise that the open-but-cautious and open-but-casual views on non-cessationism are gaining traction within dispensationalism, because they are deriviatives of the same methodology employed in the grounding of lordship salvation and limited atonement.

Finally, the disagreements in soteriology and ecclesiology accentuate the point that if dispensationalism is to arrive at consistency, it cannot ignore the methodological problems embedded in our theology. These soteriological and ecclesiological discussions need to be addressed and resolved with the same vigor dispensationalists have exerted in the eschatological debate. And we mustn't stop there. Dispensationalism needs a theological enema, to rid ourselves of the methodological σκύβαλον that so heavily influences us to place dispositive emphasis on extra-biblical authorities, and proportionally derive unsound conclusions.

We must realize that *dispensationalism is not a hermeneutic*, nor can it be our final loyalty; it is merely an explanatory device of Scripture rightly interpreted. As such, dispensationalism should be comprehensively distinctive, and not merely an alternate perspective in narrow strands of eschatology and ecclesiology. As dispensationalists, we argue that the Bible determines our hermeneutic – that it decisively favors the literal-grammatical-historical model. With that understanding must come a great appreciation for history and theology – and any other context that informs our understanding regarding the lives and times of the writers God used to place His words in our hands. But when those disciplines become our dominant influences over and against the text itself – as they have in the aforementioned areas of soteriology and ecclesiology – then we have lost our way.

Lordship salvation, limited atonement, and the cessationism debate serve as important case studies to illustrate that until we address these issues with at least some degree of exegetical finality, we will continue to be encumbered by an amalgamation theology that will continually seek to resolve to the dominant strand. Continued dispensational acceptance of TR methodology means continued acceptance of TR error.

www.ingramcontent.com/pod-product-compliance
Lightning Source LLC
Chambersburg PA
CBHW070549050426
42450CB00011B/2778